THE
KAHUNA KIT

THE
KAHUNA KIT

JOE POTTS

authorHOUSE®

AuthorHouse™
1663 Liberty Drive
Bloomington, IN 47403
www.authorhouse.com
Phone: 1-800-839-8640

© *2011 by Joe Potts. All rights reserved.*

No part of this book may be reproduced, stored in a retrieval system, or transmitted by any means without the written permission of the author.

First published by AuthorHouse   08/03/2011

ISBN: 978-1-4567-8687-8 (sc)
ISBN: 978-1-4567-8688-5 (dj)
ISBN: 978-1-4567-8689-2 (ebk)

Printed in the United States of America

Any people depicted in stock imagery provided by Thinkstock are models, and such images are being used for illustrative purposes only.
Certain stock imagery © Thinkstock.

This book is printed on acid-free paper.

Because of the dynamic nature of the Internet, any web addresses or links contained in this book may have changed since publication and may no longer be valid. The views expressed in this work are solely those of the author and do not necessarily reflect the views of the publisher, and the publisher hereby disclaims any responsibility for them.

CONTENTS

Introduction xi

PART ONE
ONE The Finder Fairy 1
TWO How the Finder Fairy does it 3
THREE The Sign Of The Three 7
FOUR Who Were The Kahunas? 13
FIVE A Day In The Life Of Joseph Potts BA 19
SIX Analysis Of 'A Day In The Life' 22
SEVEN The Three Souls Of The Kahunas 27
EIGHT The Low Self 37
NINE JO The Hysterical Computer 46
TEN Memory—Sausages In The Black Bag 48
ELEVEN Why should The Low Self worship the Middle Self? 50
TWELVE Me The Animal 52
THIRTEEN Getting To Know JO 56
FOURTEEN The Middle Self 60
FIFTEEN Smarten Up! 67
SIXTEEN When Things Go Wrong Between The Middle Self
  And Low Self 83
SEVENTEEN A Nervous Breakdown: JO Takes Over 89
EIGHTEEN The Most Important Love Affair Of Your Life 91
NINETEEN Childhood Trauma, A Block To Happiness 97
TWENTY Positive Thought Positive Thought Positive Thought 102
TWENTY-ONE The Unique Individual 106
TWENTY-TWO Getting The Best Out Of Society 110
TWENTY-THREE Positive Will 113
TWENTY-FOUR Humour 114
TWENTY-FIVE Creativity 115

PART TWO
ONE The Story So Far.. *119*
TWO Vital Force... *122*
THREE Vital Force And Hypnosis—Cutting Out The Middle Man...... *130*
FOUR Things Get Complicated.. *135*
FIVE The Mind Field... *141*
SIX Dowsing *145*
SEVEN The Joy Of Healing.. *150*
EIGHT The High Self.. *161*
NINE Getting In Touch With Your High Self............................... *175*

Illustrations
Fig. 1. The Great Gate At Tahuanaco 7
Fig 2. Further Signs Of The Three 9
Fig 3. The Tricky Relationship Of The Low Self To The Middle Self 36
Fig 4. What Makes The Lady So Strong? 125
Fig 5. The Stele Of The Lady Tuth Shea 140
Fig 6. The Kahuna System As Illustrated 142
Fig 7. The Juggler 161
Fig 8. Winged Discs And Winged Snakes 164
Fig 9. Contacting The Aumakua 176

For Julie
Who brought me shelter from the storm

Review by Graham Glynn
Dear Mr Potts,

I am writing to say how much I enjoyed reading the draft copy of **'The Kahuna Kit'** : I found it to be a most revealing study of Max Freedom Long and the philosophy of the kahunas and especially compelling in its interpretation of how the ancient wisdom can be applied by all of us living on the planet today. Whether it be the understanding and application of external healing energies or the wisdom of how to achieve peace within each and every soul in the face of contemporary problems, this text provides the answers. Indeed, it is apparent that these simple but powerful truths could mark the turning point in the way mankind relates with his **inner self**, his **fellow man** and the **planet** which sustains him ; in particular the concept of the **three selves** is of profound significance together with the eradication of mistaken Freudian concepts of a nebulous and dangerous unconscious mind and their replacement with a benign, powerful and integrated consciousness. It is this new understanding of consciousness that offers each one of us the opportunity to step forward and claim our natural birthright—freedom of **choice**, freedom of **speech**, freedom of **thought**, freedom of **feeling** and the liberating challenge of total **self responsibility**.

In my capacity as psychospiritual psychotherapist I would like to add that this book with its workshop guide will prove an invaluable tool for the layman to better understand the workings of the mind, emotions and physical body and how each can be harmonised and integrated to become good and faithful servants in the service of personal and global peace.

On my former capacity as Head of the School of Horticulture, Royal Botanic Gardens, Kew, I welcome this book because of the immense benefit that an understanding and application of Kahuna philosophy and values will be in helping mankind to rescue the planet from the brink of destruction.

Many thanks,
Yours sincerely, Graham N.C. G. Glynn grahamglynn@uwclub.net
Psychotherapy HND (Couns) ; Dip Psychospiritual Psychotherapy : Master NLP Dip : Adv Cert Ericksonian Hypnotherapy.
Horticulture : RHS., H.N.D.H., MIHORT., Nuffied Scholar

INTRODUCTION

This book is both an introduction to the discoveries of Max Freedom Long—as important for the psychic world as Newton's were for the physical world in my humble opinion—as a result of his investigation of the Hawaiian magicians, the Kahunas, updated by some discoveries of my own relating to our competitive and media-driven society, and containing a workshop which you can organise with a friend or friends, a workshop which can lead you in whatever direction you choose. Do you wish to be happy, for example? It is relatively easy to become happy once the simple but profound Kahuna system is grasped. It is a question of riding the emotional horse the Kahuna way or, as most of us do in the West, not knowing that the horse exists, panicking it and then listening in horror to the pounding of hooves on the stable door.

Characterising our inner being as purely an animal is too simple, of course. To find out some of the main characteristics of what the Kahunas called the Low Self (a much more profound concept than Freud's unconscious) the workshop begins with some simple Middle Self/Low Self body exercises which should astonish the reader and reveal the surprising character of the Great Organiser.

The Kahuna system, which I go to some lengths to explain, is knowledge which is vital to the understanding, not only of ourselves, but the entire human race. Why do we humans behave as self-sacrificial mothers or saints, dedicated artists, robots, demons of destruction or binge-drinking slobs? More confusingly, these roles can be interchangeable within the individual: the great artist can double as an irresponsible sociopath while the binge-drinking slob of Saturday night may put himself in great personal danger, rescue a child from a burning house, and become the hero of next Wednesday. The modern science which characterises us as mindless machines doesn't know the answer to these paradoxes and Freud, who believed the unconscious mind is basically wicked and destructive, didn't know the answer either; the Kahunas did, however!

Our souls are comprised of a trinity and the astonishing variety of our behaviour, from the sublime to the downright horrific, simply depends on which part of that trinity we plug into. By referencing historical records and demonstrating how the three selves make their presence felt in a typical day I shall make the Kahuna Trinity of Mind seem self-evident in its history, simplicity and subtlety.

The workshop is interwoven with the explanatory text; having grasped the Kahuna system it is for readers to choose the area most significant for themselves. Would you like to access that CCTV camera within which is one aspect of our Low Self? Do you need to control that emotional volcano of yours? Do you want to achieve happiness? Would you like to improve your memory skills? Or do you need to improve the rational skills so essential to the Middle Self as captain of the psychic ship? Do you wish to become a real healer?

The truths of the Kahunas as revealed by Max Freedom Long are surprising ones, revising our accepted beliefs about spirituality. Spirituality is not just a matter of floating away on an etheric cloud. The Low Self, the emotional volcano with all its faults and desires, provides us with the vital force, an energy which has been ignored by modern science, to reach the High Self, the God Within and is essential to our physical and mental well-being.

'As Above, so Below' to quote the famous Emerald Tablet.

The Kahuna system with its three souls, three soul bodies and three variant vital force energies numbers ten elements if we include the human body which houses these nine elements. It seems a complicated system but, fortunately, I discovered a famous crop circle which, as perfect in its way as the London underground map, gives a detailed representation of all aspects of the Kahuna system and enables us to see at a glance how it all works.

This book can lead to psychic development. Having achieved happiness and linked the two lower selves as inseparable friends united in the face of the battle of life, there is magic to be found within the Kahuna system—for being on good terms with your Low Self is as important to your psychic development as it is for your happiness. Indeed, to take control of our thoughts and think positively is to put our first foot on the ladder of psychic development and magic practice!

I will be eternally grateful to Max Freedom Long because it was through following his description of how the Kahunas healed that I myself became a powerful healer. In case you don't know it, as I didn't myself, real healing is a spiritual power which can miraculously cure conditions that have resisted conventional medicine for years, a regular, homely miracle. I include an account of my healing experiences together with the Kahuna system of healing.

Healing utilises the miraculous, 'atom-smashing' (as Max put it) energies of the High Self, the God Within, and the Kahunas help us all to inch closer—or if you're very lucky make giants steps closer—to this divine force which, unbelievably, we all share. The discovery of the Aumakua or God Within is the most wonderful golden nugget of knowledge that Max mined from the Kahuna system.

There is a logical accumulation to the exercises in the book but feel free to explore any exercises that take your fancy and don't worry at all if some of them don't work.

WORKSHOP EXERCISES

Let's start with some simple, amusing but rather amazing exercises 1-5 which are ultimately the route to happiness and magic.

You may well find that exercises in this book have life-changing consequences as they did for me but, if some don't happen for you, don't worry; everyone's different, just pass on to something that works.

1. *No one likes to be criticised but this is ridiculous*.................*xvii*
2. *Criticisms in general* ....*xix*
3. *Allergies, a useful medical tool* ....*xx*
4. *God*.................*xxii*
5. *Winning*.................*xxiii*
6. *The Finder Fairy*................. 2
7. *Write your own Day in the Life* 25
8. *Dr Emile Coué's magic mantra:* 45
9. *Anaesthetising pain.* 47
10. *A memory game.* 49
11. *Discovering your Animal Self* 55
12. *Examining emotional baggage* 82
13. *Loving JO* 96
14. *I'm so lucky* 100
15. *Reclaiming your own* 109
16. *Sensing vital force* 129
17. *Magnetic movement.* 133
18. *Getting To Know Jo With The Pendulum* 148
19. *THE KAHUNA SYSTEM OF HEALING* 158
20. *Controlling vital force* 174
21. *Contacting your Aumakua.* 179

Exercise 1

To do these eye-opening exercises you will need the help of a friend.

(a) Extend your strongest arm with the palm up and the elbow straight.
(b) Your friend will now try to push down your arm by pressing on the palm of your hand while you will exert as much strength as you can to keep your arm straight. This will give you the average reading of your strength. Sometimes people's arm strength is so feeble that the friend can push it down with two fingers or even the little finger.
(c) Say, 'I am a wonder' and get your friend to test your strength.
(d) Say, 'I am a wanker' and get your friend to test your strength.

The strange implications of Exercise 1

It really is astonishing how praise (c) keeps ones' strength up and ones' arm straight while self criticism (d) turns the aforesaid arm into jelly no matter how hard we will it to stay up. We may want that arm to stay strong but, despite our best efforts of willing its strength, it goes all floppy on us if we abuse ourselves.

I've seen strong men struggle against this reaction. They want to demonstrate their male superiority and show they're not falling for a trick which belittles their sense of control and independence of mind. Alas, having declared themselves a wanker they just cannot keep that arm straight, much as they want to.

There are clearly two parts of our mind at work here—the part of our mind that we are directly aware of and says, 'I'm not going to be fooled by this silly trick and my arm will remain strong' . . . and miserably fails to have its orders carried out.

There's another part of our mind lurking in the background that is really in control of our body.

Which part of our mind is reacting to the above stimulus?

Certainly it is hard-wired to our bodily strength.

It has nothing to do with our conscious will of the moment. What we consciously want will not work on it.

Freudians would claim that this is the unconscious mind at work but here's nothing unconscious about the above reaction. It's decisive and immediate as if some highly sensitive inner being is listening to what we say and pressing a button to give us strength or take it away, irregardless of what we wish.

Interestingly, I have met only one man on whom these exercises don't work who an his wife describes him as a 'resister'; prolonged exercise of will power over many years in testing circumstances has eventually overcome the reactions of his Low Self.

The Kahuna Kit

Exercise 2
Criticisms in general

> (a) Think of something nice to say about the government such as 'what generous handouts our wonderful government gives us' and test.
>
> (b) Think of a criticism of the government such as 'these people are destroying our freedoms' and test.

The implications of Exercise 2

Even though the effects of Exercise 1 are astonishing at least there's a certain logic to it as none of us likes to be criticised and it seems logical that we might go a little floppy in the face of criticism. The result of Exercise 2, however, where we are criticising not ourselves but the government, is most peculiar. Our arm goes all floppy when we criticise the government (or governance as they prefer to be known) and we all know as we're alert, free-thinking people that these characters need as much focussed criticism as we can bring to bear on them. So what on earth weakened us in the case of Exercise 2 and turned our arm to jelly?

Why did that little person below press the weak button because the government was criticised?

Exercise 3
Allergies, a useful medical tool

    (a)   If you think you've been drinking too much booze recently hold a wine bottle in one hand and test the strength of your other arm as before.

    (b)   If you suffer from skin problems test while holding cow's milk—even an empty carton will do.

    (c)   Test anything you think you might be allergic to.

Implications of Exercise 3

Did you go all floppy with the wine test? Perhaps you've been overdoing it and that hen night out with your girl friends was the final straw. Don't worry too much because an allergy is not necessarily for all time. Give yourself a couple of weeks off the booze and try again and hopefully you can keep that arm up and continue modest social drinking.

Remember: drink is a good friend but a dreadful master.

If you go floppy on cow's milk then it's perfectly possible that your skin problems come from drinking it and eating cheese and chocolate. We were never really meant to drink stuff meant for calves containing their growth hormones. But if we give up cows milk what to put in the tea and coffee? I think soymilk tastes like liquid cardboard and soy products have their own side effects. I have found goat's products a satisfactory substitute for cow's milk and when I had my cholesterol test recently (by the way, ask doctors for a lipid profile if you want a cholesterol test, a balance of good and bad cholesterol, and stun them with your medical knowledge) the result was so low they couldn't believe it and took it again.

It seems that this little person pressing the button knows all about our bodily health.

Kinesiology, whereby the practitioner talks to your body through a responsive weak/strong wrist is based upon this reaction, as are most allergy tests. Scientists would call the person inside who knows all about your body's health the autonomic nervous system.

This is a useful DIY allergy test. Allergies, however, can be a complicated business and it's a good idea to seek medical advice rather than relying on this alone.

Exercise 4
God

    (a)   Extend your arm, palm up, say, 'God is great' and get a friend to test your strength.

    (b)   Extend your arm; palm up, say, 'God is gross' and have a friend test your strength.

Implications of Exercise 4

This is a bit of a shock. Oh no! It seems the person in the recesses of your mind pressing the button has strong religious convictions. He or she believes in God and although you, the rational you, may be a confirmed agnostic, the person with their finger on the button goes all floppy when He is criticised.

You thought you'd put all that superstition behind you. You can dimly remember a vicar bleating away in the pulpit, trying to make you feel guilty for even thinking about sex. 'God is listening to your thoughts,' bleated this idiot. You've learned of the intellectual dishonesty of your traditional religion, its lack of historic evidence and its terrible record on human rights. You've seen right through the whole religious fraud and moved on to healthy, guilt-free New Age beliefs.

And now you find that a part of your mind is frightened of God! Oh no! What a disaster!

Exercise 5
Winning

    (a)   Extend your arm, say, 'I will win the national lottery' and test.
    (b)   Extend your arm, say, 'I will never win the national lottery' and test.

Implications of Exercise 5

    This is getting stranger and stranger and more than a little worrying. Darn it! You don't even gamble! You think the national lottery is nothing more than a con with that ad of the big hand of the Lottery God zooming through your window and pointing at you the winner. Tell me another! The chances are 14 million to one against you winning it! Then there's the government spending the lottery money taken from the suckers on all sorts of dubious projects.
    That's what you think as an informed person!
    But you went all floppy when announcing that you will never win!
    What are you really?
    An egotistical religious nut who wants to gamble his or her assets away?

ONE
The Finder Fairy

Dear reader, you've been so patient doing the tests and experiencing their worrying results and implications—though all will become perfectly clear and not at all worrying shortly—that I'm going to give you a treat and show you what happens when you get that person below working for you.

Do you have a problem finding things? There was a time when my house would ring with my desperate inquiries because an outing or the completion of a job was maddeningly thwarted by a vital missing object—"Julie! Where are my keys? Where's my wallet? Where's that book I have to take back to the library? Where are those screws I took out of the radio?"

"Joe! Your wallet's on the mantelpiece where you left it."

"Oh! So it is!"

"It was right in front of you."

"Oh."

"And your screws are under your wallet."

"Oh."

These desperate conversations are no more!

I find my own.

And it's all due to my discovery of the Finder Fairy.

Exercise 6
The Finder Fairy

You know about snapping your fingers as people used to do to swinging jazz?

(a) Can't find your keys or anything else for that matter?
(b) To summon the Finder Fairy snap the two middle fingers of your right hand with your thumb three times.
(c) Call (or think if you're very shy and don't want people to regard you as mad), 'Finder Fairy.'
(d) Wander around in an aimless sort of way.
(e) There they are on the fridge.

TWO
How the Finder Fairy does it

The results are positively magical. Wallets, door keys, pens all turn up obediently. Once I dropped an irreplaceable screw in the garden, sent in the Finder Fairy and immediately saw it glinting in the grass. Last Monday I went to a huge car boot sale. One of the things I wanted was a filter jug. Thousands of items are bewilderingly on show, asking likely stallholders got me nowhere, I was hunting the proverbial needle in the haystack and so I sent in the Finder Fairy. Sure enough, I turned back and looked over a stall which I had already examined and there was a superior filter jug for sale.

If the Finder Fairy can't immediately find the missing object, just relax and wander *aimlessly* from room to room where the fancy takes you, until voila!

That religious nut and gambling maniac down there certainly has an awesome eye.

It seems that looking at stuff as we normally do we're wearing blinkers. We see what we *want* to see or what we're *programmed* to see.

Life itself programmes us. For example our image of someone when we meet them for the first time is crucial as to how we perceive them in the future. So if we first meet a friend when he or she is smiling and jumping out of a large car that image will stay with us during the relationship, even though they may fall on hard times, cease smiling and buy a small car. It's the same with movie or rock stars. Know your hero when they're young and virile and an action male like John Wayne could go on blowing the bad guys away and knocking them flat until he was practically at death's door.

Female sex-bombs have a much shorter screen life and today age-obsessed critics scrutinise even male stars like maniacal plastic surgeons touting for business though someone with Jack Nicholson's charisma can carry on to death's door making lots of boring movies. Tom Jones with that amazingly powerful voice intact still remains a sex symbol.

Our perception of reality is strangely unreliable. It must be very difficult for the police examining witnesses to a crime, as it's a recognised fact that, although these witnesses have witnessed the same events, without being bribed or wishing to deceive, they report quite different details. From a personal point of view don't you find in the aftermath of an accident or any traumatic event it's sometimes difficult to remember exactly what happened? I'm a careful driver leaving lots of space between my car and the car in front but I once clipped the rear of a vehicle at a traffic junction and it was hard to remember how the accident had actually occurred, just what had made me take my eye off the bumper of the car in front. As we want it to be the other person's fault in such a situation, we instinctively skew the evidence in our favour as undoubtedly the other motorist does to incriminate us. 'No, he didn't signal before pulling out to the right . . .'

Of course, politicians and admen are constantly manipulating what we see. At a famous summit meeting the 'youthful' President Reagan didn't need an overcoat on a winters' day, unlike the 'sickly' Mr Gorbachev who was wrapped in overcoat and scarf.

However blinkered at we may be in our everyday perceptions, him or her below has got a darned security camera at their disposal. They miss nothing and they've got it on tape. It's said that under the hypnosis, which accesses him or her below, you can remember who was standing at a bus-stop you drove past twenty years ago.

So we above who, for example, have to give evidence in court, are wearing blinkers.

While him or her below has a security camera and tapes it all.

It's a worrying situation because those seeking to manipulate us can appeal to him or her below who misses nothing while the blinkered folk up here haven't a clue as to what's going on.

It's called subliminal advertising. The adman shows material which is recorded only by the security camera below. We think of subliminal advertising as a frame in an advertising film which is too brief to be perceived by us above but is faithfully recorded by him or her below. You could have a frame showing a sexy image in the middle of an ad for soap to make it especially attractive, for example. We above won't perceive the sexy image but the soap will seem mysteriously sexy and attractive to the

CCTV person and we'll buy it. Scandals have occurred involving this sort of thing and subliminal advertising is supposedly banned.

Subliminal advertising doesn't have to involve film, however. Ads placed around sporting events are subliminal. Frequently their contents have nothing to do with the sport taking place and the viewer might ignore them. That security camera is taking it all in, however, and making a totally ridiculous association between fags and sport and concluding that tobacco makes you run faster.

Sometimes the cunning admen bribe even buskers to help launch a new product. As we struggle home on the tube and think of the evening meal we above ignore the words sung by the busker. Our security camera doesn't, however, and, if we are not careful, we will find ourselves mysteriously drawn to a new product we see on TV.

On UK TV at the moment (2008) there is a very clever and somewhat sinister chap called Derren Brown who brilliantly illustrates the power of that security camera below. He invited a couple of admen to his studio (whom we watch taxiing there) to create an advertising campaign (about a pets' cemetery, if I recall correctly) and handed them a brown paper envelope, which they had to keep safe. As instructed, the duo spontaneously created a campaign and were then asked to open the brown paper envelope and—blow me down with a feather!—there was a description of the advertising campaign virtually the same as the campaign the duo had created of their own free will.

And how was this 'magic' achieved?

Well, we watch again the journey of the admen to the studio in their taxi and there outside on placards or posters were the main elements of the campaign that they 'spontaneously' generated. While the blinkered minds of the admen censored the placards and posters as irrelevant their security cameras below recorded everything and, when the moment to create an advertising campaign arrived, wrote up this suggestive material of their own free will.

The Finder Fairy is the security camera working for us. It's magic!

Happy hunting.

Before we can explain just why you seem to be a religious nut, obsessed with winning the national lottery, who finds criticism of the government depressing, it's necessary to give you some background to the Kahuna system.

I am profoundly grateful that I discovered the Kahunas through the writings of Max Freedom Long. In all my psychic researches nothing has been of real practical importance except the Kahuna system which I use all the time.

We can start our inquiry by asking ourselves about the significance of the Sign of the Three. Have patience. It may seem a little abstruse but believe me, it's highly relevant to our inquiry.

THREE
THE SIGN OF THE THREE

All is divided in three parts
The emerald tablet of Hermes Trismigistus

Fig. 1. THE GREAT GATE AT TAHUANACO
James Churchwood was puzzled at the many references
to three in this astonishing monolith

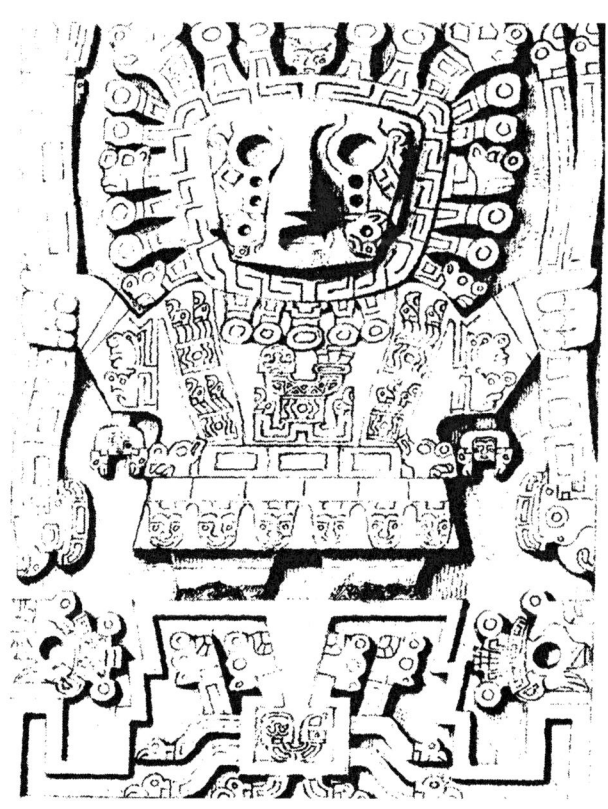

I would like to draw your attention to the obsession of the human race, especially in a religious context, with the figure three.

The references to a trinity are manifold and begin with the first recorded religions. The equilateral triangle, which of course has three sides, is one of the most ancient religious symbols. A pyramid contains equilateral triangles. To the Chaldeans Ensoph the Creator was symbolized by a triangle and a triangle can be seen over the altar of old Catholic churches.

Incidentally, symbols—be it triangles, pentagrams or crosses—are not inherently good or evil in themselves. Magic is judged to be black or white depending on the *use* to which it is put; the same magical energy would be good if it were used to heal and bad if it were used to kill. Similarly, the meaning people burden a symbol with and what use people put a symbol to determines whether it's good or bad. A crucifix in the hands of an Inquisitor is a symbol of evil. As we know, the Nazi swastika was for centuries a Hindu symbol of good luck and perhaps will return to that meaning in the fullness of time.

In looking for historical signs of the three we in the West are all too familiar with the trinity of the Father, Son and Holy Ghost and you may well have asked yourself what on earth it's all about.

The God of the Egyptians consisted of Shu, Set and Horus.

The Hindus assert that there are three gods designating the one God, Agni, Indra and Brahma.

The Greeks believed in a trinity of Phanes, Ouranos and Kronos.

In Guatemala the godhead is divided into Bitol the creator, Alom the engenderer, and Quhalom who gives being.

In Peru the Creator Pacha-Camac was head of a trinity involving, himself, Con and Uiracocha.

The trinity is built into Druidic thought. The Gaulish gods were threefold: Taranis, the Thunderer, Teutates the tribal god, and Esus, the Lord—a sky god, a tribal god and a personal god. Their three moral precepts were. 'Worship the gods, be manly and truthful.'

The Chinese have a trinity of Qin Shi Haung Di, Confucius and Loa Zi.

The great gate at Tiahuanaco (Fig. 1) could have been built nearly twenty thousand (yes, 20,000) years ago, according to Colonel James Churchward (And why not? Stone is impossible to date).

Churchward was very puzzled by the significance of the number three and the fact that it had been woven into the Great Gate so many times. Three fingers instead of four, three tears on each cheek, a face made of three levels etc, etc. The search for the Sign of the Three throughout the archaeological evidence that remains to us is a fascinating affair. The reader undoubtedly can multiply the evidence I have collected a hundredfold. It's a lot of fun!

Fig 2. FURTHER SIGNS OF THE THREE

There can be little doubt that the three fishes at Wrexham Priory represent the Christian Trinity of Father, Son and that puzzling figure, the Holy Ghost. The actual occult significance of the Trinity is unknown to the average Christian but at least we can establish that the trinity is enshrined in a triple image here.

The Trinity is also interwoven with Celtic culture as we can see from the three-horned bull (Fig 2e). The Celts could undoubtedly count and a bull with three horns is a puzzling image if it doesn't have some occult significance. The three-headed god (Fig. 2d) is highly suggestive of the Kahuna system of three souls. The Celts were obsessed with making stone images of the human head and carved several tricephalos—round stone heads with three faces.

Hollowed out of the dry earth in the Pisco Valley near Nazca are the 'Three Crosses' as the Spaniards call them. The image, which has puzzled everyone, seems to be related to the Mexican 'Tree of Life', a triple candelabra displayed at festivals and decorated with a goddess, birds and angels. Here again we find the sign of the three—as we do at the Trilech of Newgrange. Of course, it is purely speculative to suggest that these trinities were a reference to the three souls but, when we look at the manner in which the trinity is enshrined in every religion known to man, cumulative evidence provides a plausible reading of these otherwise enigmatic symbols.

Now I don't wish to suggest that the pyramids were built purely to celebrate the trinity. They were probably constructed to concentrate vital force for purposes we can only speculate about, having lost touch with the ancient technology, a technology needed to accomplish the miracles of building the pyramids or even carving hieroglyphs in granite—the latter feat, archaeologists would have us believe, was carried out using only bronze tools (okay, mate, you do it!). However, if you are going to construct a vast energy device why not build into it sacred numerology enshrining precious occult knowledge which must not be lost to mankind? There are two sets of three at Giza, the small Queen's pyramids and the great pyramids.

Why is there this obsession with three throughout history?

I believe it refers to the Kahuna belief that *we have three souls*. This is not just a religious myth but also a working system of psychic knowledge. The Kahuna trinity gives us a plausible explanation for the recurrence of the three in the Great Gate and throughout pre-history and history—occult knowledge so precious, so essential to comprehending the human soul, to magical practice, that it must be written in stone. To the worshipping masses the trinity would have a popular but non-informative meaning of the Father, Son, Holy Ghost sort, or whatever suited the particular culture.

We have not one but three souls.

The Jewish Qabalah is constructed of trinities and it's surely no accident that Jewish writers such as Freud and Marx employed such a system in their thinking. In Marx's case it was a historical trinity whereby history was supposed to inevitably 'progress' from capitalism, socialism towards a communist utopia. As is now apparent, the socialist, 'scientific' view of history has been overtaken by events in the real world. It was just a scientific myth to mislead the ever-gullible human race.

In the 20th Century Freud, inspired by the Jewish tradition, came up with his own trinity of mind—the ID (the unconscious, a maddened brute), the EGO (the conscious self) and the SUPEREGO (a sort of muddled social worker whose chief job was to tell the EGO that Mr Freud was right whatever the evidence). Freud claimed, quite falsely, that his was a scientific system, just as Marxism was supposed to be a scientific theory of history.

The Qabalah incorporates the trinity of *thesis, antithesis and synthesis* to explain all phenomena, including the declension of the unknown Godhead into the physical world with its inevitable compromises and pain.

The Kahuna system would function within the Qabalah system as follows: the God Within, the joyous *thesis* where all is resolved, all is one, all is joy, produces as its own *antithesis*, the Low Self. The Low Self is struggling within the material plane, fragmented into a separate ego, a separate body, and a separate sexuality and is tasked with enabling the body to survive and reproduce so that we can win. Connecting the two is the *synthesis*, the Middle Self, the Clever One who has to moderate between the two major souls, the God Within and the survivor below, the saint and the animal.

This is by no means an easy task. A person who threw in his lot entirely with the High Self and determined to do no harm to man or beast or insect or lettuce would die to the physical. Indeed, certain yogis, having attained enlightenment, could then see no further purpose in living. Equally one who entirely throws in their lot with the Low Self and, wanting to feel good all the time, drowns the pains of existence in alcohol, drugs and indulgence can also die an early death. To lead an enlightened life on planet Earth, satisfying the needs of subsistence while paying homage to the God Within is a subtle and paradoxical affair.

When William Blake wrote that 'The road to excess leads to the palace of wisdom' he was joking.

'Nothing in excess' from the Delphic oracle is certainly a better guide to longevity at least.

Should we take an interest in the latest views of the scientific white-coated devil on the map of the mind? Actually, I'm not opposed to science per se but only those worshippers of scientism who bring us, with many a fanfare, the technology of hell instead of the technology of heaven. An honest scientist is an important citizen but frequently unemployed as most scientific jobs are in 'Defence' or Big Pharma.

Dr Paul McLean, head of Laboratory of Brain Evolution and Behaviour at the national Institute of Mental Health in the USA, concluded that there are three regions of the forebrain in higher vertebrates. The midbrain he thought of as the reptilian, rather like writer John Cowper Powys's Ichthyosaurian ego, the dinosaur enjoying his mud bath, equivalent of the Low Self. Surrounding the mid-brain are the limbic system and the neocortex. The limbic system is for emotions, perhaps the physical seat of the High Self, while we reason with the neocortex.

These white-coated devils are not our best guides, however. Their theories change all the time and are rigidly confined to materialism. Sacred knowledge has anticipated all of their so-called discoveries and is a better guide to our personal salvation, not to mention the future of the human race itself.

FOUR
WHO WERE THE KAHUNAS?

Before we can get any further I must introduce you to the Kahuna system, the psychic knowledge that I had the good luck to discover in a book called 'The Secret Science Behind Miracles' by Max Freedom Long.

Max Freedom Long's epochal discoveries were made in highly exotic circumstances. When he took up a teaching post in Hawaii in 1917 he became fascinated by the magic practices of the Kahunas, the local fire-walking magicians who were reputed to heal, kill, talk to animals and even change the future.

The Kahunas were the high priests of a Polynesian cultural and racial group who inhabit an area stretching from New Zealand to Hawaii and Easter Island. How they came to occupy this land remains conjectural to this day. Max argues convincingly that they came from the Near East while Thor Heyerdahl demonstrated with his raft *Kon Tiki* that they could have floated there from South America. The jury is out as it is with so many of the problems of ancient history. We really don't know how the human race originated, why we built vast stone structures—some of which can't be reproduced to this day with our advanced technology. Isn't it extraordinary that the purpose of such a huge object as a pyramid remains incomprehensible to modern science? Even how such a common foodstuff as wheat appeared in our agriculture is a complete mystery. Which hunter-gatherer could have decided that a certain grass would make wheat if carefully bred and nurtured for several generations? Indeed, why would a hunter-gatherer want to do any such thing?

Certainly the Kahunas established a sophisticated society based upon psychic knowledge and when Europeans first made contact with the Polynesians who were on their best behaviour it must have seemed they were landing on a mysterious tropical paradise of happy, sexy natives whose only job was to peel a banana—especially when one considers the shameful conditions of the poor in eighteenth century England. But all was not entirely as it seemed. The Polynesians are a robust people and the competitive, testosterone-driven urge of the male wrought its usual havoc with tribal and factional fighting.

When Captain Cook landed in 1778 on Kauai the appearance of the British Unidentified Floating Object naturally had the effect of a UFO landing on the White House lawn. The Kahunas who made contact initially thought Cook was a god and sought to use him to boost the cause of their own faction, just as the President might chum up to a UFO crew to show the Russians that he had important new friends. The Cook episode soon went pear-shaped, however, as he stayed long enough for the Kahunas to realise this was no god but just a nasty Brit. When the English sailors were ordered to snatch the Kauaian king for some petty misdemeanour (imagine the fuss if a Hawaiian war canoe sailed up the Thames and tried to arrest George III!) lusty warriors took out their war clubs and spears, got to work on the non-godly Captain Cook and cooked his goose.

Max Freedom Long gives a romantic description of fugitive magicians. The Kahunas were not all sweetness and light, however. At the time Genghis Khan was ravaging Asia a Stalinist Kahuna called Paao invaded Tahiti and set up a menacing Kahuna dictatorship forcing the real healers and shamans to take to the hills. And, as Max noted, certain Kahunas, who acquired a sinister reputation and were understandably feared, specialised in killing with the death prayer.

The Tahitian magicians also shared the perennial danger posed by any priesthood who enjoy a life resembling that of a perpetual student. A priesthood doesn't work for a living, enjoys an often spurious social status and naturally comes to fear that the public will one day wake up and its privileged lifestyle will be snatched away. The priesthood's answer to this unpleasant possibility is to strengthen its hold on the population by tightening the mind-forged manacles of superstition.

As Paao realised there's nothing like a bit of human sacrifice to keep the population in order. Imagine some priests telling you, "You're such a wonderful person, Jo."

"Thanks very much."

"The gods love you above all others, Jo."

"Pleased to hear it. Hope they bring me more wives."

"They love you so much they want to eat you and we're sacrificing you next Sunday. Be thankful for this great honour."

"Ohohoho . . . er . . . lovely." It wouldn't do to be ungrateful to the Gods.

Sacred knowledge and genuine religious impulse inevitably gives way to politics and most priests forget what real mystical insight or magic is all about after a generation or two.

By the time Cook arrived idols and taboos proliferated in the land of the Kahunas and, if your shadow fell on the king this counted as psychic assault and you got the chop. Women, as the physically weaker party, were laden down by taboos and even forbidden to eat bananas in public as it was too suggestive. Undoubtedly if priests fancied an area of the island they could make it taboo for the rest of the population and also devise sexual taboos and rituals favourable to themselves.

Then, of course, a new priesthood arrived, the Christian missionary whose desire to bestow God on the ignorant savage was only equalled by a desire to steal that savages' natural resources. The Kahuna Hewahewa, ignorant of the lessons of Captain Cook, seeing Unidentified Floating Objects make landfall on Hawaii, concluded, as you would, that these newcomers must have powerful magic on their side. To ingratiate himself with the invaders he ordered the destruction of all idols and temples, thus obliterating Hawaiian religious traditions and creating a cultural vacuum. The missionaries came ashore and Hewahewa lined up a few sick people. "Okay, Christian magicians, if you'd just like to heal these guys . . ." And, of course, as Hewahewa realised too late, the Christians had no magical ability whatever and, far from befriending the Kahunas or taking any interest in their culture, the invaders, for their own commercial reasons, made it a criminal offence to be one.

What kept Kahuna practice alive was that some Kahunas could still kill you with that nifty death prayer and so no Hawaiian cop was going commit suicide by arresting them.

As the Kahunas were banned, Max Freedom Long had at first a frustrating time trying to meet them or learn about them. Then he had an exciting breakthrough when he contacted one Dr. William Brigham, curator of Bishop's Museum in Honolulu, an elderly scientist who knew from experience that Kahuna magic practices actually worked. Kahunas had once taken him on a fire-walk across a stream of barely-cooled lava, for example. Dr. Brigham, frightened by the heat of the lava, which from the bank felt as hot as standing beside an open oven, timidly asked them if he could keep his sandals on. The Kahunas roared with laughter and gave him a push onto the baking, flickering surface. Although Brigham safely crossed the lava his footwear exploded in the heat—to the further amusement of the magicians. Dr Brigham quite correctly felt the Kahuna magic could be of vital service to humankind and was desperate to find out how it actually worked.

Max himself had some interesting sessions with Kahunas who, ban or no ban, flourished behind the scenes. On one occasion Max went with a friend to visit a Kahuna who told Max he would soon have a bad traffic accident. What would you do in such a situation, clever reader? Max Freedom Long was a quick-witted guy and he pointed to his friend and asked if the friend would have an accident too. When the Kahuna said his friend was safe Max decided to keep him as a driving companion.

Sure enough a few days later Max was about to cross an intersection when his friend called out for them to stop! Max had failed to notice a large truck, which would have smashed into his car, and his friend saved his life.

Despite his diligent researches, Dr. Brigham, no further forward in uncovering the secrets of the Kahunas, died a disappointed man and Max left Hawaii in 1931 no wiser as far as the secret science was concerned.

Then in 1935 he had a breakthrough, which I believe is as important on the psychological and psychic level as Newton's apple was for gravity. Max suddenly realised that the solution to the problem had been staring him in the face. The Hawaiian language is built up of root meanings. The Kahunas must have had words for the elements of their magic and the missionaries who had notated Kahuna prayers recorded these words. These prayers thus held in coded form the basis of Kahuna beliefs.

After decoding the magic practices of the Kahunas (a word which, ironically enough, means 'Keepers of the Secret') Max discovered that, *not only do we have one soul, we have three.*

Max discovered that what Freud called the unconscious, that part of us that scripts our dreams and controls us by stealth, which he refers to as the Low Self the Kahunas called the *unihipili*. The word could be broken down into several root meanings. *Pili* means a spirit, which attaches itself to another and acts as its servant. *Nihi* means a spirit that does things carefully and secretly but—wait for it—is afraid of offending the gods—as you discovered with Exercise 4.

The Middle Self, the thinking one who we regard as us, was known as the *uhane*.

The most extraordinary discovery of the Kahunas is that we have a God Within, our third and most amazing soul, the *Aumakua*.

There is no substitute for reading the works of Max Freedom Long in their entirety as they detail just how the Kahunas worked their magic illustrated by many a fascinating anecdote. Max, in addition to decoding Kahuna prayers, compared his discoveries to magic practices around the world, thus building up a complex picture of magic in action. He then formed the Huna Research Association to try and reproduce these magic practices.

I have been unable to discover a biography of this great psychic researcher, whose ideas are so important for our self-knowledge and psychic future, and, in the only photograph I have seen of him, he looks like a bespectacled bank manager. He must have been quite a guy, however, as he lived with three women—presumably one for each of his souls.

A huge question remains: from whence did the extraordinary magical system of the Kahunas, a system which puts Freud and Jung to shame, a system of working magical practice, actually arise?

How are you with speculative archaeology, inquisitive reader? Personally, I find it a lot more interesting than those academic conmen who count out history in spoonfuls of dirt from a dig and claim to know exactly how the pyramids were built. According to Colonel James Churchward, author of 'The Lost Continent of Mu' (A book which makes some interesting arguments for the existence of the Pacific Atlantis, Mu) the existing, scattered Pacific islands are nothing more than remnants of that large continent.

Easter Island would be fragment of a once great continent instead of a tiny island inhabited by demented and superhuman natives who chopped down every tree to transport the massive statues which they spent every minute of their lives frantically carving. If once situated on the shores of a continent, however, the sombre carvings with their baleful stare would have had their place as sentinels to intimidate the invader. Their round hats could well be symbols of the High Self indicating that this was a continent inhabited by dangerous magicians.

The extraordinary knowledge of the Kahunas supports the theory of Mu. Clearly a bunch of witchdoctors marooned in the middle of the Pacific couldn't dream up a highly-sophisticated system of psychic knowledge,

knowledge relating to the *sacred knowledge* of ancient cultures across the world, knowledge which puts modern thinking into the shade, all on their own. If the Kahunas were descendents of survivors of a priesthood belonging to an ancient continental culture then their possession of such an extraordinary psychic system of working magical knowledge makes perfect sense.

Incidentally, according to Kahuna folklore the sacred knowledge was brought from the Pleiades by a race of space pigmies who, after fighting it out with the dinosaurs, settled on Mu. Well, that's one explanation for the origin of the species—no more implausible than the Theory of Evolution whereby a monkey shed its fur, agility and ability to produce vitamin C and, in a blink of cosmic time, without leaving any fossil traces of the missing link, became a creature capable of destroying its own planet. Without wishing to embrace creationist beliefs, I do feel that it's time for open debate on this fascinating problem about which everyone, Darwinists included, can only speculate at this moment in time.

A writer friend of mine informs me that she met impoverished Kahunas in Hawaii who were living as beach people despite possessing great spiritual power. In a world culture that has no concept of true spirituality this is tragic but hardly surprising.

Before we examine the three souls of the Kahunas, which could be referred to as Me, Myself and I as they are all aspects of us, I give you a day in the life of Joseph Potts BA. He thinks of himself as a philosophy graduate and environmentalist but who's really in charge of this character?

FIVE
A DAY IN THE LIFE OF JOSEPH POTTS BA

Joseph Potts BA is awake and relieved to be awake because he was about to be arrested—in his dreams. How welcome is the real, wide-awake world of the familiar bedroom and slumbering, faithful companion! He was about to be arrested for growing apparatchiks in his garden. What unutterable rubbish and how had he ever believed it? What was that horrible dream about anyway? The ridiculous dream had started with a policeman knocking at the door, Joe remembers . . .

My God, a copper! What does he want?

"Hello, sir. You are Mr Potts?"

"Yes, officer. Do come in out of the rain. How can I help you?"

"Your shoe licence has run out, sir and your new shoes have already clocked up half a kilometre over the limit. I'm afraid I'm going to have to fine you two pairs of Wellies."

"Two pairs of Wellies! Sorry, Officer, there's just so much to think about these days. I just forget my shoes were unlicensed. Cup of tea, officer?"

"Don't mind if I do, sir."

But then . . . As the copper is drinking his tea Joseph Potts looks out of the kitchen window and . . . Good God! The rain has washed the soil off the latest corpse he's buried in the vegetable garden . . . the rotting hand of his wife is shining in the rain . . . If the cop looks out the window . . .

"Just come and sit down in the porch, officer and we'll sort out the fines . . ."

"Nice cuppa, Mr Potts. But aren't you growing apparatchiks in the garden? They're been illegal since 2004 . . ."

"Those are West Indian artichokes, officer, not apparatchiks."

"There looked a bit like apparatchiks, sir. "

Joe Potts

This utter nonsense was nerve-wracking during dream time and spoilt a night's sleep as Joseph frantically distracted the policeman from seeing the exposed corpse . . .

But now he's awake wondering how he could ever have been stressed out by such utter, drivelling nonsense.

What a relief to be awake! Oh there's that Greenpeace letter on the bedside table. 'Must send them a cheque . . . Nice crate of red wine I bought on offer yesterday from the supermarket . . . fruity, vanilla aftertaste . . . Still haven't sent Greenpeace a cheque . . .' Joseph rises and looks at himself in the mirror. 'Looking good. But why is it that cameras always make me look so fat? Damned cameras have got it in for me!'

Then, as he's eating breakfast, a shadow falls over our still sleepy hero. Only yesterday Joseph bought a car from a nice, white-haired neighbour, Mr Winkle, but there's an ominous knocking in the engine. 'Pray God it's not the big end going! £500 hasn't vanished down the drain, has it? Perhaps Mr Winkle just left his shoe under the bonnet.' Joe's not very good with cars and hasn't found out how to lift the bonnet yet. 'Or is the bloody thing a dud?' Joe's breakfast, which normally floats smoothly down to the stomach, sticks in his gullet at the thought of poor Joe being landed with a useless car! 'Swindled! Old bastard!' A spasm of rage makes Joseph chew his cheek as well as the toast. 'Damn it! Ow! Not my morning!'

"I'm just off to my garage to see about that car, darling," he says to his partner later.

As Joseph walks down the road to his car he bumps into Mr Winkle himself.

"Sure that engine's all right?" He asks impulsively. "Seems to be knocking a bit."

"Well it was all right when I had it," replies Winkle warily. "Buyer beware, you know."

'Surely Winkle is joking? Is there a hard look in his eye? Can't be, can it? He's a nice neighbour. The car will turn out OK. Fuss over nothing.'

Joseph drives off to his garage, smoothly handling the clutch pedal, clutch, brakes in a complex rhythm as he thinks about the incident. '"It was all right when I had it," said Winkle. Perhaps he just meant it's a good car. Perhaps the knocking is harmless after all. It'll be all right.' But why does Joe have this sinking feeling like £500 pounds in notes is just slithering away down his stomach?

"Hello, mate" says Joseph to his mechanic. "I was wondering about the car . . ."

"Big end's going, Joe. Heard it coming down here. Want me to dump it for you?"

"No thanks. I'll take it back to the bastard who sold it to me!"

Joseph drives the car back home. Old Winkle has taken him for a ride! That 'buyer beware' was no joke! 'The old git has robbed me! Buyer beware! Winkle beware! Gonna grab the old git by the throat and . . .'

Now what's happened? Joseph has taken the wrong turning at the roundabout. If he's not careful, he'll find himself on the motorway instead of back home! As he turns back along the bypass he's in the wrong gear, grinding at the clutch. HOOT! He has been crawling along the fast last and a bloody motorist hoots him. 'Calm down, Joe. Keep your mind on the road! Forget Winkle for the time being! Before you have an accident.'

Joseph is back on the outskirts of town when—*Screeeeeech!!!!!* A limo has just braked in front of him nearly causing a crash. Joe has slid to a halt inches from the elegant rear bumper. 'Who is this bloody fool?' Joe is pumping with adrenalin. He flings open the car door and springs like a cat onto the pavement. This idiot is going to get a load of abuse. Joe is bouncing with anger when the owner of the Limo lets down his electric window. 'My God! He looks like a Kray twin crossed with a crocodile! What on earth are gangsters doing here? There's four of them in the car! Jesus!'

"Whayawant?" Drawls the limo monster.

"All right, mate?" Croaks Joseph. His mouth has gone dry, his knees are weak and he feels a bit sick.

"I want to buy some fags," says the monster. "D'ya have a problem wiv that?"

"All right, mate," croaks Joe idiotically and hobbles back to his car on jelly limbs.

'What a morning!' Thinks Joseph Potts BA. 'I must go home, have a cup of tea, calm down and figure out what to do next. I must be calm as I approach Winkle. I don't want to grab him by the throat and get arrested.' later as Joe is sitting in his back garden in the evening sun listening to the birds he is overcome by a sense of peace and wellbeing. 'What has all the fuss been about?' he thinks to himself.

SIX
ANALYSIS OF 'A DAY IN THE LIFE'

The dream. The night before Joe watched 'The Curse of the Zombies' on TV in which the dead dug their way out of their graves—hence the buried hand. Joe also has a parking fine outstanding and the two have got jumbled up in dreamtime.

The surreal quality of dreams has been noted by your adman who nightly creates Dalíesque spectacles to go with the TV dinner. Why do panthers become cars which become marching robots every night on TV during the commercial breaks? In this bizarre world the consumer marches through skyscrapers which fall like discarded washing or he cracks the world, which turns out to be a mirror before marching through to consumer superpower.

Utter tripe as this might seem to our reasoning self, as the adman knows only too well, it is the visual currency which the Low Self is familiar with every might in dreams. Clearly society's manipulators think the Low Self dreamer is a more reliable consumer than the Middle Self making a reasoned choice.

It seems that a part of Joseph Potts's mind, philosophy degree or not, will believe any old surrealist rubbish. If the Fat Man from Fartland threatens to blow up the Planet Earth in dreams then Joseph Potts B.A. will worry himself silly. Credibility is like a label, which can be attached to anything at all while we're dreaming. (And how much better off are we when awake, we may ask ourselves?)

There is then a part of Joe's mind that jumbles up what he's seen on TV with his daytime problems and replays them at night. While dreaming Joseph Potts BA can be persuaded of anything, but anything, at all.

Freed from the torment of nightmares Joe wakes into a world of high self-esteem. He thinks he deserves a good day. Sees himself in the mirror as slimmer than he really is. He spots the Greenpeace pleading letter which, associating one thing with another, only makes him think of the excellent crate of wine he has spent £30 on.

His teeth normally chew food, which slithers happily down into the Joe stomach. The thought of losing £500 changes this, however. Joe chews his cheek as well as his toast which seems to stick somewhere in his gullet instead of slithering down.

It seems there is a part of Joe's mind that *organises his bodily functions* such as eating and digestion. These functions can be disturbed by strong emotion.

When thinking about Mr Winkle Joe gets 'that sinking feeling'. It seems that part of Joe knows more about Mr Winkle that Joe does. Joe drives off with the effortless and complex co-ordination of eye, feet and arms needed to drive a car, none of which decisions and activities require verbal control. He doesn't have to say to himself: "Now you must depress the clutch pedal before braking or you will stall the engine." He can listen to music or conduct a conversation with a passenger while driving the car.

The reasoning mind—which likes to think of itself as the real Joseph Potts BA, the one and only Joe—can think about problems while a complex series of actions are being performed without fuss by another part of the mind.

Joe has *the Great Organiser* working for him. The Great Organizer has mastered an entirely unnatural activity such as driving a car. It will drive the car for Joe while he is engaged in other activities.

The Great Organiser is truly great. For example, a motorist will view the task of driving on the 'wrong' side of the road in foreign lands with horror. To the reasoning mind the task of driving the wrong way round roundabouts and making an unimaginable left-hand turn across two lanes seems impossible. Foreign driving is pure horror to the reasoning mind. Yet it's amazing how quickly the Great Organiser takes over this seemingly impossible task.

Yet the Great Organiser has his limitations. Joe learns the terrible news! The car is rubbish! His violent thoughts overpower the Great Organiser! He finds himself driving in the wrong direction, in the wrong gear, in the wrong lane! *The Great Organiser is vulnerable to strong emotions.*

Joseph must calm down before he has an accident!

A calmer Joe is driving into town when . . . not Joe, but the Great Organiser slams his feet to the floor. Joe screeches to a halt inches away from the Limo which has suddenly braked in front of him. Joe can smell smoking rubber. The Great Organiser then floods Joe with fight or flight adrenalin as he jumps out of the car. Faced with the gangster, however, the Great Organizer wisely provides him with jelly limbs and dries up his vocal chords.

NOTE: The Great Organiser *is fully awake and alert* and is using Joe's body or he couldn't slam the brake to the boards before Reasoning Joe has barely registered the fact.

NOTE: The Great Organiser is fully in charge of Joe's emotions as our hero leaps out the car to confront the limo driver. His Great Organiser has a strong sense of self-preservation and doesn't want to fight it out with a car full of gangsters.

Let's face it, reader. Our rational consciousness, our Middle Self, is only the tip of the iceberg. Out of sight, swimming in the waters of consciousness below, is another we, the Low Self.

NOTE: Joe has made two positive Middle Self choices. Firstly he has decided to calm himself down before having an accident on the bypass. Then, burnt out by the shock of near-collision and meeting a car full of gangsters, Joe makes a second positive choice. He will not rush round to Mr Winkle and seize him by the throat. Joe will calm down and think rationally about what to do next. Before making these positive choices Joe has been a prisoner of events, a Low Self who only reacts to external stimuli.

But who is this character inside that controls our digestion, drives our cars, plays our instruments, floods us with emotions?

Far from being unconscious this driving force is watching through our eyes every moment of the day!!!!!!!!!

Far from being unconscious this inner personality dreams while the Middle Self, tired with coping with the real world, is asleep!!!!!!!!

Day and night, what Mr Freud called the unconscious, a term which has become enshrined in common language, IS NEVER UNCONSCIOUS!!!!!!!

IF THIS LOW SELF, IF THE UNIHIPILI, THE ME, IS NEGLECTED OR MISTREATED, DEPRESSION AND, ULTIMATELY, ILL HEALTH IS BOUND TO RESULT.

There is a third aspect of our mind, however, which Joe accesses at the end of the day. Frequently associated with the beauty and harmony of nature this aspect of our mind suggests a higher consciousness, known as the High Self by the Kahunas. His car problems become trivial as Joe, enjoying this higher mental plane, realises that, after all, it's good just to be alive and a car is just a car.

Exercise 7
Write your own Day in the Life

Write an account of your day from waking to sleep and analyse the hidden forces at work which determine your behaviour.

If you're one of those people who think they don't dream keep a notepad and pencil at your bedside. As soon as you wake write down what's in your mind and you'll find it's a part of your dream. You'll then be able to remember the rest of your dream when you look at this note in the morning. Don't get hung up over dreams but they're an interesting insight into your Low Self at play. Whereas Freud baldly stated all dreams are wish-fulfilment you might find like myself that The Great Organiser seems to include a surprising amount of self-torment in dreams, which are frequently much worse than the day that preceded them! Occasionally the surreal gibberish of dreams can throw a light on our deep relationships.

(a) If a dream is an important message coming from the High Self you'll know it.

(b) Note how your rational Middle Self and Low Self interact. When it comes to good intentions, whether towards the environment or other people, see who gets the better of you—The Great Organiser or The Clever One.

(c) Remember this is an exercise in self-knowledge and we have to understand ourselves if we are to control ourselves. Be honest even if you have to burn the account.

SEVEN
THE THREE SOULS OF THE KAHUNAS

Know thyself
Written on the Delphic oracle

So isn't it essential to know ourselves, to know what really makes us tick? How could you repair a car if you didn't know how it worked? How can you repair yourself if you don't know how you work?

The three Kahuna souls discovered by Max Freedom Long, were:

1. The *unihipili* (pronounced oo-nee-hee-pee-lee), known as the Low Self, the animal self' or the unisex JO.
2. The *uhane* (pronounced oo-hah-nay) known as the Middle Self or the reasoning self.
3. The Aumakua (pronounced Ah-oo-mah-koo-ah), which is the High Self or the God Within.

We frequently feel such a powerless and insignificant atom of modern society that it is surprising to think we possess a God Within—yet this astonishing discovery of Max Freedom Long is true.

I sometimes refer to the Low, Middle, and High Self, as *Me, Myself and I* as they are all part of us. In a sense they are different stages of our psychic development. They are all us but they have widely differing and yet complimentary functions. 'The Low Self' sounds as if a person is harbouring a foreign invader. However, Me is a unique part of our unique personality.

It's not all that complicated. As 'A Day in the Life' has demonstrated in the book, a little self-observation will reveal to us the existence of the three souls.

In some respects the "Me" of Me Myself and I is an utterly brilliant bio-computer controlling our memory and bodily functions and, as Max

Freedom Long comments, isn't 'low 'in the sense of being low quality at all.

How we relate to the Low Self is profoundly important to not only our happiness but also our health. Most of the healing I do is hands on healing which may cure a long-standing back problem in one healing session. However, I have also begun to use the Kahuna map of the mind to treat people mentally and the effects can be dramatic. Once people realise that their happiness is a question of how the Middle Self relates to The Great Organiser and that they have *considerable control over how they feel* depression can just vanish overnight and neuroses can be swiftly combated.

In youth we struggle to impose ourselves on society and need the three souls working in harmony to achieve success. Inner harmony also makes us much more resilient in coping with the surprises and shocks of the rocky road of life.

The High Self is beyond our comprehension and yet can also take over our window of consciousness in moments of creative inspiration or spiritual exaltation. We can also focus the High Self through the window of consciousness with certain meditative exercises as I shall show. So, although in adulthood the Middle Self takes us over for most of the time, the three souls are in a dynamic relationship—sometimes a disastrous one as when the Low Self seizes control, sometimes a magical experience of enlightenment as when we contact our loving High Self.

Me, Myself and I have functioned in a dynamic relationship from the hunter-gatherer phase of human activity until present day society with its bizarre technology. How does our Low Self cope with social restraint? Why do we sometimes become the reverse image of whom we really are? Why does such a large section of the population follow football and become severely depressed when England loses yet again? Why do some of us, while leading timid non-violent lives, enjoy violent images on screen? What happens to the Low Self in war? What is a nervous breakdown?

Some people are instinctively close to their Low Self whereas others are ruled, superficially at any rate, by the reasoning Middle Self. The Middle Self, frequently hogging the window of consciousness and bolstered by social role and education, seems to *be us*, to comprise our identity. Yet we are more than our job. The Inner Child remains very powerful even in scientific people who consider themselves ruled by fact and reason.

The Low Self is not some foreign force in the personality like the Freudian Unconscious but is *us*, our individual soul with its own inherited abilities and character.

When we are children our Low Self is at one with the world, out on the street. Our life is all lives, our mother is all mothers and our house is all houses. The Low Self is very vulnerable during the innocence of childhood and can easily be warped due to lack of parental love or early challenges of school. I have found it interesting to illustrate problems of this nature by the lives of the famous who bob about on the ocean of celebrity. Marlon Brando in his autobiography illustrates the horrible emotional legacy of abusive parents and the lasting damage such self-obsessed slobs do to the Low Self of their children.

Modern day society, with attention-grabbing technology living in our pocket ready to take charge of our consciousness at any moment of the day, also has a profound effect upon our Low Self. Is that mobile phone friend or foe? Never before have so many of us 'ordinary' folk in the West been so relatively well off and in possession of such amazing technological toys. Yet psychologists all observe widespread depression and lack of self worth. This is largely because we are so bombarded with celebrity images that this tantalising vision of success, so near on the TV yet so remote from our humble lives, leaves many of us with cripplingly low self-esteem. We just can't help comparing our poor, little, woefully insignificant lives with those huge Elvis-sized lives dangled in front of us day in, day out.

I will show you how to escape from this fatal habit of mind.

How can we best cope with the stresses of modern society? How can our Low Self best cope with the technology of the moment? Is society our soul enemy? Is its function in the West to leave us with both a huge overdraft and an inferiority complex to match? I believe our relationship with modern society is a complex one and that it's important for our well being to understand this relationship in the round and use it to our best advantage.

The Middle Self has the awesome power of will and choice. Myself can choose to join the army and take poor JO into a war zone, to take an extreme example. Myself is the boss of Me and makes all the decisions great and small. The Low Self, sometimes called the younger brother or sister soul by the Kahunas, worships the Middle Self and does everything it can to help The Clever One.

Sometimes, however, Me and Myself have such different approaches to life that a situation can arise where the right hand literally doesn't know what the left hand is doing. Ecology is a subject which illustrates this conflict only too well. The Low Self likes nothing better than a stroll in the country or along the seashore as nature both soothes the senses and reminds us of the High Self. However, JO's immediate physical and social interests are frequently at cross-purposes with the environment.

We need a house, need warmth, need work, need food, need sex and our Low self is greedy for success. Myself, the logical one, might see the point of being Green but JO is relentlessly driving towards, not only fulfilling needs, but chasing success, wanting an even bigger family, house and car. Who doesn't know the intelligent women sincerely concerned about the planet who goes on to have a third or forth or fifth child? The broody urge of their JO just got the better of their ecological concerns. Sometimes even ecologists deny that overpopulation endangers the planet. It seems that a Low Self love of the human species has blinded them to the findings of ecological research.

Our Low Self wants to win and competitor JO wants not only a house, food and sex, but a BIG house, the BEST food, sex with as MANY partners as possible, a BIG car, a BIG reputation and MANY children.

Which ecological writer worries about the trees pulped to sell millions of his books or worries that his books seem to effect human behaviour so little? Does Al Gore worry about the air travel necessary to expand his highly profitable Green career? I don't think the conflict between the Low Self and the Middle Self over ecological matters is easily resolved but at least the Kahuna system helps us understand just why we are so hypocritical when it comes to saving the planet.

The current ignorance of the Inner Child is a collective and individual disaster. We still believe our JO to be a slumbering, unconscious Freudian beast which can only be accessed after ten expensive years on the couch or we don't think of our Low Self at all. This can have dire consequences for our mental and physical health. Sometimes we ignore JO and drag him or her into intolerable work situations and eventually our Low Self, feeling consistently abused and thoroughly unsafe in the hands of what should be its older and wiser brother or sister, will strike back. We can be immobilized by depression, mysterious complaints and pains and, eventually, an actual physical disease.

Sometimes the Low Self can just misunderstand what we want in the real world, does its best, and inflicts terrible neurosis. It has enormous power!

Nothing so clearly reveals the wonderful or terrible power of the Low Self than hypnosis. (See Part Two Chap 3 for an analysis of how hypnosis actually works.) A hypnotic subject's flesh can be painlessly pierced and wounds won't bleed as Derren Brown revealed by hypnotizing Robbie Williams and skewering his arm on TV in 2006.

The sinister Svengali, Derren Brown, in another TV show in 2007, without putting the subjects into an hypnotic trance, so manipulated the Low Selves of suggestible subjects that three out of four business trainees attempted an armed robbery! He had turned their Low Self into a criminal sleepwalker.

Initially, they thought they were attending a business workshop where Brown would empower them to be successful and he did teach them a few mental tricks and gave them a plastic gun as a present. Their repressed Low Selves were delighted to learn that they had to *Go For It* to be successful. They also had cross the bounds of legality by stealing some sweets from the store opposite their pub meeting place. Having stolen a packet of wine gums the Low Self of these previously law-abiding types felt an enormous sense of excitement, relief and empowerment!

The security camera belonging to their Low Selves also recorded the mysterious green van photograph on the wall of the conference and took on board the 'Go For it' message of a Michael Jackson song while their blinkered Middle Selves ignored these details which were to play a crucial part in their criminalization.

As far as their reasoning Middle Selves were concerned the charismatic Brown was empowering them with techniques to escape their inhibitions, defeat their business rivals and become a huge success like him. They were taught to down a colleague by 'projecting vital force' in an exercise which Brown said was purely suggestion. (An irritating feature of Brown is that he mimics genuine psychic phenomena.) They were involved in a scientific experiment where they had to train a subject (fortunately an actor) with painful and finally lethal amounts of electricity to see if electric shocks would improve the subject's learning skills, all in the name of science. (Incidentally, this sort of exercise reveals how most of the cruelty in the world is *socially* inspired rather than being an individual choice; none of the subjects would have chosen to electrocute someone off their own bat.)

This conditioning process on the Low Self came to fruition when the subjects were sent walking down a London Street which had been cordoned off for the sake of the experiment. They were subjected to various triggers such as a passing car playing the Michael Jackson conference song and an ad with the slogan GO FOR IT. Suddenly . . . there before their conditioned, greedy, opportunistic Low Self eyes . . . was the green van recorded by the inner security camera which had been popping up all over the place . . . and a guard carrying bags of money. Their Low Self now knew that success lay in transcending legality, in going for it, in making the most of this supremely exciting opportunity which fate had thrown in their way, a challenge which, thanks to Derren Brown, they were now empowered to accept. Three out of the four chosen subjects pulled out their plastic guns, ordered the guard down on the floor, snatched the money bags and made off with their prize—only to run into a crowd of people including the evil Derren Brown.

You would think this form of TV entertainment was highly traumatic for the subjects concerned, especially to the vulnerable Low Self who had been so horribly tricked.

The show did demonstrate very graphically that we do have a Low Self who notices and remembers stuff that the Middle Self regards as trivial, who comes to Low Self conclusions about right and wrong and who is quite capable of performing a dangerous action which is totally out of character!

It's not only Derren Brown who is leading us astray, however. Society itself is constantly urging the Low Self to do daft or dangerous things, such as borrow too much money or join the army. And we go for it. We have a personal national debt of a trillion pounds while ordinary people ruin themselves by wasting thousands on such trivial pursuits as chat lines or quiz shows. High rollers like Colonel Parker lost millions gambling. How very important to realise that we have a Low Self, that Myself must be in charge of this wasteful character who is so easily led astray and that we must work in harmony with our Inner Child! This book will show you how to do just that.

The truth about Me and Myself and getting to know and love Me is easily understood and enables us to both understand and to take charge of ourselves emotionally and physically but Max Freedom Long's discovery of the High Self, the Aumakua is perhaps the most exciting discovery of all. The third soul, however, the High Self, is as far beyond the comprehension of Middle Self as the Middle Self is superior to the Low Self in reason. This causes huge problems when we try to describe mystic states—the same word can have hugely different meanings if it refers to a spiritual rather than a rational category.

Mystics sometimes claim that we possess 'the God within', that we have a 'hidden treasure' within our minds. It can seem very unlikely indeed to a modern person; as we struggle to earn a living or vegetate before the TV it seems ridiculous to suggest that these minds of ours, stuffed like a supermarket shelf by education and the media, can contain a God. I will show, however, that the God Within concept is not so far removed from our common experience as you may have thought. Amazingly, the God of the Kahunas *does* exist within us and the Aumakua *can* be accessed by us to our inestimable benefit.

The High Self is the Guardian Angel Spirit, the spirit involved in healing, the white light above, the God of the Kahunas who we can access to a greater or lesser degree. Such abilities as healing or clairvoyance are accessed through the Aumakua. The High Self is the gateway to our psychic future.

'Working with the Trinity of Mind' provides readers with the techniques of achieving happiness. Readers should be able to get in touch with both their Low and to a lesser extent their High Self. A dowsing pendulum, for example, is a useful tool for getting to know the Low Self. The pendulum can also access information from the High Self if one is so attuned.

Some of my patients have found it an emotional experience to recognise their inner brother or sister, the secret slave and helper who has been neglected all their lives. It's vitally important to forge a loving, mutually helpful relationship with the Middle and Low Self as our everyday happiness is based on this relationship. You can be as successful and intelligent as Marlon Brando yet live in a meaningless and destructive emotional world if you have a damaged Low Self and don't relate to it properly.

The Low Self also plays a hugely important role in our physical health as the placebo effect, whereby the doctor essentially hypnotises the patient back to health, demonstrates.

The Kahuna system, as discovered by Max Freedom Long, is a huge gift to the world. It actually enables the human race to understand itself simply and clearly for the first time. The interplay between our emotional, competitive, greedy JO and the clever, reasoning Myself (sometimes given to intellectual arrogance) explains so much about our behaviour. What we call hypocrisy is simply the competition between the Low and the Middle Selves of our personality. The Low Self wants a crate of wine and buys it with the money which should have gone to Greenpeace. This doesn't stop the Middle Self continuing to pontificate gravely upon ecological matters while drinking the wine.

Neither the Great Organiser nor the Clever One can have it all their own way. The Low Self has to concede to some of society's demands. The Middle Self can never be a purely rational machine as even its 'rational' conclusions are driven by the emotional demands of the Low Self. No wonder we get a little confused. In A*n Essay on Man* the 18th century satirist Alexander Pope describes the human race in a strangely relevant manner.

'He hangs between; in doubt to act or rest;
'In doubt to deem himself a god or beast;
'In doubt his mind or body to prefer;
'Born but to die, and reasoning but to err.'

Throughout the poem Pope describes what is almost a Kahuna system, including an incomprehensible God above who yet achieves a miraculous order of nature while we vain humans strut our disastrous stuff below.

According to the Kahunas we are *both* God and beast, the Low Self and the High Self, linked together with a golden chain of Vital Force, while our reasoning self, the Middle Self, negotiates between the two. But, alas, *we reason but to err.*

The Middle Self should be the Clever One, Myself should be captain of Me, but Myself frequently reasons only to make the most disastrous mistakes—such as our scientists believing to this day in all seriousness that we are nothing but mindless machines. As for our philosophers! These clever gentlemen spent over 100 years puzzling over how the thought 'Raise your arm' could make a person raise their arm!

'They reason but to err,' as the poet so wisely said. From the eighteenth to the twenty-first century little has changed. There's no one who can be quite so foolish as a clever person.

As this book is about the Trinity of Mind and includes my own humble take on the Aumakua of the Kahunas, the God Within, inevitably the question of *magic practice* arises. How is it that healers can heal and clairvoyants can predict the future?

Anyone who has known a good clairvoyant will know that *sometimes* they *can* predict the future. I used to know a well-known local clairvoyant Madame Bernadette as a friend. When I was living by the seaside she predicted, much to my surprise, that I would leave but retain connections in the area. That's exactly what happened. Although the prediction seemed totally meaningless at the time my family soon broke up, I left the area and returned regularly to see my girlfriend's parents. Bernadette also told another friend that her trust fund was being swindled and she should change her solicitor. The information proved to be true. My friend was totally ignorant of being robbed when she consulted the clairvoyant so the information wasn't in her mind. So much for the fabled 'cold reading', whereby the clairvoyant questions the credulous subject and reads their body language, by which sceptics vainly attempt to explain away the phenomena of clairvoyance!

The great Max states that everyone can be a healer. Is this actually the case? As I am a healer myself I have personal knowledge of the matter.

Max also introduces us to the Kahuna system *for making successful prayers*. Clearly, if we could make successful prayers this would be a valuable ability to say the least. There was a popular system recently of writing a letter to the Dear Cosmos (I believe Noel Edmonds, a gruesome TV presenter, found it worked and he now graces our TV again) which promises something similar. Interestingly enough, as a young child Uri Geller practised a technique similar to that advocated by Max. Geller visualized things he wanted, such as a puppy, and sure enough his dad appeared with a puppy in a box. For Geller it was like having an Aladdin's lamp in his mind.

What he was doing is a process of visualisation and prayer described by Max Freedom Long. Of course, he is Uri Geller. Can we learn to do the same?

From the point of view of personal stability and happiness the Kahuna system is indeed a precious gift. Everyday happiness is happiness of the Low Self and the Low Self is perfectly accessible. The Clever One just has to take charge of the Great Organiser and all is well for the Inner Child can easily be soothed and cheered. Congratulations on having chosen to read this book, astute reader. Undoubtedly, in some cases you will obtain more benefit from the Wisdom of the Kahunas than even I did.

Fig 3. THE TRICKY RELATIONSHIP OF THE LOW SELF TO THE MIDDLE SELF

The left brain doesn't know what the right brain is doing!

EIGHT

THE LOW SELF
GETTING TO KNOW ME
MEET THE 'ME' OF ME, MYSELF AND 1
THE UNIHIPILI OF THE KAHUNAS
THE GREAT ORGANISER
SOMETIMES KNOWN AS JO

'I admonish thee, whoever thou art that desirest to dive into the inmost parts of nature; if that thou seekest thou findest not within thee, thou will never find it without thee.'
Abipili, an Arabian alchemist

Remember exercises 1, 2 & 4

The Great Organiser *who operates an amazing CCTV, hates being criticised, hates criticism in general and goes all wobbly at the thought of criticism of God.*

These were surprising results weren't they, puzzled reader? Why object to justified criticism? And this lingering fear of the Almighty is mighty worrying when we thought we'd put that sort of thing behind us.

One great advantage of the Kahuna system is that it reveals the character of him or her below. Meeting your *unihipili* is like meeting a person. This is not some weird Freudian unconscious that has been imported into the psyche and needs ten expensive years on the couch to access. It's a soul—your soul. A character armed with a security camera is watching through our eyes, seeing a helluva lot more than we do, drawing his or hers own conclusions, immediately reacting to whatever life throws up but unfortunately can be manipulated by the likes of Derren Brown or worse.

Remember: *If you don't control your Low Self somebody else will!*

From exercises 1 to 3 you have learned that Me, JO, the *unihipili*, is very sensitive and *hates* criticism, especially of God. Won't have it!

However rational we think we ought to be we are superstitions beings.

Here is Kevin Contemporary BA off to get a job as structural engineer for 'Megabuild'. Kevin is an atheist, a liberal, a man of the 21st Century who believes that modern science is the cutting edge of reality. As he springs along the pavement towards his interview, however, a wizened gypsy jumps in front of him on her crutch and waves a worthless sprig of heather. "Heather, love?" She whines. "Good luck from a gypsy?"

Although theoretically sympathetic to all ethnic minorities Kevin, anxious to keep his appointment, brushes her aside and hears an angry snarl behind him. Has he been cursed? A cloud seems to come over him and he almost wants to turn back and tip her. It's too late to turn back, however, and he finds himself stumbling under a painter's ladder. It means seven years bad luck on top of the gypsy curse. His ridiculous sense of gloom deepens.

Kevin doesn't get the job, his car is vandalised when he gets back to it and he feels within himself that it's all because of the gypsy's curse—though he doesn't confess this shamefully ridiculous idea to anybody.

JO is both highly superstitious and God-fearing and those Kahunas knew why.

'*Nihi*' from U*nihi*pili, Max discovered, means a spirit who is both secretive and careful and is *afraid of offending the gods*. This is crucial information concerning the character of the Great Organiser, the soul easily influenced by superstitious fear and guilt, for if the Low Self has been persuaded that it has offended God it will fail to function properly.

Even if you are a scientist and atheist, superstition lingers in the Low Self. Give the most determined atheist a fatal disease and he or she will soon be clutching lucky charms and praying to God. Send Richard Dawkins to Iraq, get the Taliban to launch a firefight in his direction and he will soon be praying to whatever God he can dimly remember.

GOD

The word itself is likely to resound in your mind, vulnerable reader, whether you say 'I don't believe in Him at all' or 'I feel I must go to confession this week'.

The Kahuna Kit

Needless to say, the natural superstition of JO has made the human race easy prey to priests of all religions over the years. '*God wants you to do X*,' remains a potent instruction. But why does the Great Organiser fear God so much?

Is JO just superstitious? Is it just some sort of mental baggage that we humans have picked up from primitive times when we thought thunder was God shouting angrily at us?

OR DOES THE LOW SELF KNOW MORE ABOUT GOD THAN MIDDLE SELVES DO?

WE SHALL SEE!

Why were we enfeebled in Exercise 5 at the thought of never winning the national lottery when we never buy a ticket anyway?

It's because JO is desperate to WIN! WIN! WIN!

"Yeah!" The triumphant raised fist of the sporting champ. "I won!"

The orgasmic spurt of champagne.

It's an irritating cliché of TV as ecstatic winners splash the bubbly into the dust.

Yet like many an irritating TV cliché it refers to a basic characteristic of JO.

Picture the following scene. Old Mrs Pompous-Superior is in town to get some painkillers and another bottle of oak-matured whisky. Has the hip operation worked? That hip still gives her the gyp but she's damned if she's going to walk with a limp in front of all the hoi polloi. She fixes a smile which resembles a rictus of pain on her face, bravely swings out and comes to the *Big Issue* seller. 'She may be a young girl but she's common and very poor,' thinks Pompous-Superior and feels a little glow at the thought of her own massive share-holdings. She buys a *Big Issue*. The girl selling the mag gives a broad smile and thinks, 'The old bag may be loaded but I'm young with my life ahead of me.' They both look down the alleyway at a toothless tramp grinning in the sun and wrinkle their noses with humorous distaste. Meanwhile the tramp is thinking, 'Ah, de ladies. What will dey ever know about life? Dat time I won de bare-knuckle boxing contest of Derry Fair and de place went wild! Dat's living for yer! What will dey ever know?'

If children play competitive games these frequently end in cheating, quarrels or fights as their JOs angrily react to losing. Adults are much more circumspect in competition. They may not fight if they lose but it still depresses them. Social life itself is a form of competition on which the consumer society itself is based. My house is bigger than yours, my car is newer than yours, my child is brighter than yours . . . even my *refuse* is bigger than yours (Yes, the inner Me can even feel proud of its production of bulging bin liners as if these are elephant droppings indicative of a more powerful animal.). I'm prettier than you. I'm more ecological than you. Educated men will become competitive about their knowledge. Healers will compare the power of their vital force.

Have you ever found yourself lured into a game of football, tennis, croquet, cards or Monopoly? Isn't it surprising the amount of excitement such a challenge can arouse without even a penny being at stake? If we win our energy bubbles like champagne whereas if we loose it runs away like dish water down the drain!

When we win we've got the attention that the Low Self knows he or she really deserves. Shucks, it was easy but we did it. We won! We're not making much of it but we're a winner! Perhaps this winning will reach out into other aspects of our life. Successful men are as intent on winning at games as they are winning in business. I used to know a man called Joe (and later Lord) Kagan who made a million out of manufacturing a peculiar raincoat. Joe played chess with an alcoholic neighbour and always stood an unopened bottle of whisky on the shelf facing his opponent to distract the poor man from his chess moves.

Winners are singled out, they're everybody's friend, they get attention and attention getting is a basic human hunger. Incidentally, a most important means of loving your child is to show them attention for without attention we are screaming into the void.

Unfortunately, mugging a person also gets their attention. The bullies, the vandals, the criminals are also seeking and getting all the attention they need from their victims.

Road rage is also related to the competitive urge of the Low Self. JO, while driving the car over a long journey, will come more and more to occupy the window of consciousness. The Low Self doesn't like losing and being overtaken will make him or her feel like a loser. We are all hard-wired to WIN WIN WIN whether we acknowledge the fact or not. Therefore any rival motorist that cuts us up is the focus of vengeful Low Self rage with sometimes spectacular and blood-spattered results as JO springs out of the gridlocked car to right the wrongs done to him.

Ain't it a bitch! Most of us hardly win at all. Statistically, there are bound to be a helluva lot more losers than winners in society, millions of them in the case of the National Lottery. In almost every field there are millions of losers to every winner and most of us are left with that down-the-drain feeling whether we try to win at work, win the lottery or play cards.

How do we cope with losing all the damned time in our lives? One trick is to transfer our competitive instinct onto some group with more chance to winning than we have. We can join a football club and howl on our team with all our hearts. "A family's a family but football is serious," says the obsessed Geordie football fan. The sound of a football crowd in full cry is the sound of a whole stadium full of JOs baying for the success they crave. This desperate urge to Win! Win! Win! can easily spill over into football violence as JO has put a lot of hope and energy into the 'noble game' and the competitive urge is linked to aggression.

Aggression projected outwards is violence. Aggression projected inwards is depression and, when England inevitably loses the World Cup yet again, those fans who've so robustly bayed for their national team feel deeply depressed—to the point of needing medication or attacking their wives in some cases.

Sometimes we transfer all this desperate competitive urge to the firm we're working for: 'Yeah! We got the contract!' Regan presidential aides determined to 'Win one for the Gipper' sometimes went too far and found themselves in the clink after the Watergate scandal instead of being part of a triumphant team.

So desperate are we to win that we'll go to a race meeting because the royals are there, hoping that some of the royalism will rub off on us. (The royals would never do anything so foolish; instead they cleverly bestow worthless honours on the successful in order to associate themselves with success). The citizen of a powerful country, though his wife kicked him out and he's on welfare and he can't remember when he last won a game of draughts or anything else for that matter, will still feel a throb of pride when his country is bombing some other person's country. He doesn't understand what it's all about but it must be good because it's 'my country kicking ass'. Only when his welfare is cut because too much money has gone to the war effort will the patriotic citizen doubt the excellence of the war.

Gambling is essentially fuelled by the desperate competitive instinct of poor JO. 'He's the men who broke the benk of Monte Carlo.' The silly old song expresses every punter's dream as does the hopeful assertion—'I'm gonna bust Las Vegas!' The punter's Low Self is so desperate to be a winner, desperate that his own personal magic will overcome the cards, the wheel, the God of Chance that while he is losing a fortune his JO will fiddle the betting losses so that his rational self hardly knows how much money has gone down the pan until it's too late. 'I'm gonna win! I feel lucky tonight!'. Music to the ears of the casino.

Like it or not, the competitive instinct is hard-wired into our Low Self and pre-Freudian writers such as Herman Melville were keenly aware of the fact. "There is something in us," Melville wrote in 'White Jacket'. "Something that, in the most degraded condition, we snatch at a chance to deceive ourselves into a fancied superiority to others, who we suppose lower in the scale to ourselves." Melville was thinking of a white sailor feeling superior to a black sailor but this desire to feel a cut or two above others applies *within* all races as well as between them.

Gentle and considerate reader, have you ever been really kind and helpful to a friend in trouble? And then this friend, this treacherous so-called friend, when back on their feet, far from displaying any sign of gratitude, dropped you or even attacked you! It hurts doesn't it?

This is the work of their JO. 'It feels good to help a friend when they're having problems through so fault of their own,' you think innocently. Unfortunately, your kindliness has transgressed against their competitive instincts. 'She's only giving me help because it makes her feel big,' thinks the friend's competitive JO instead of being grateful. 'One day I'll show her that I'm better than her.' Many of our relationships founder on just such misunderstandings. You have to be a mature person to feel gratitude these days for our individualistic egos have been pumped up to bursting point by a media which is in league with our conceit.

Our sexual, financial and social needs satisfied then we only raise the competitive stakes. Fame is now the Spur. William Blake drew an amusing cartoon of a little man with his ladder on the moon, entitled 'More'. He was right.

Both personally to obtain happiness and as a species, we must at least recognise our competitive spirit, deal with it and twist it to our own advantage.

According to Exercise 3 the Great Organiser knows all about our allergies.

In fact, the Low Self is a bio-computer of genius who is in charge of our mental and physical health.

Nothing demonstrates the power of the Low Self over our health than the placebo effect which was initially discovered through of drug testing. Incidentally, I am certainly not opposed to modern medicine per se. Before antibiotics people such as Field Marshall Montgomery's unfortunate wife could die from an insect bite which had turned septic. Antibiotics, although they can affect the stomach flora in some people and lead to severe health problems, have saved millions of lives, including mine.

Not all modern drugs have the magic efficacy of antibiotics, however. And how would you test a new drug on people, anyway?

In the early drug tests they decided to give one group of patients the new drug and another group of patients an inert pill which looked the same as the real drug. As a double blind they made sure that the doctors in the research project didn't know which drug was the real one. Then, of course, the wonderful new drug would cure so many patients (In those far off days doctors innocently thought of curing rather than merely treating a disease) while the fake drug would have no effect at all.

The first drug research project of this sort must have been a profound shock to the doctors taking part. Because a third of patients taking the dummy pill were cured! This bewildering turn of events was called the placebo effect! These darn placebo patients even developed imaginary drug side effects known as the nocebo effect. The astonishing results were first published in 1955 in a paper called 'The Powerful Placebo' by H K Beecher and have puzzled the medical establishment ever since. Doctors know that it works but can't understand why it works. Recently I met a woman whose high blood pressure was dramatically reduced during a drug trial . . . by a placebo . . . and now she's taking the real thing.

And not only drugs produce the placebo effect. Fake operations for heart problems or acute joint pain whereby only a superficial scar is left on the patient also achieve astonishing cures. Hearts improve and agonising joint pains disappear.

It's thought unethical to trial with placebos in the case of serious illnesses such as cancer and therefore we don't know whether those who survive cancer treatments do so thanks to the placebo effect rather than the toxic drugs and radiation.

What is happening here? How can a placebo pill rival the work of the latest product from Big Pharma? The answer lies in the character of our Low Self. Our friend JO is watching with awe the witchdoctor in the white coat as he advises on the new pill or recommends the operation. "Right," says JO after the magic pills go down. "That's the asthma sorted!" The Low Self promptly inserts a new programme into the bio-computer and health results. It is very important that the doctor believes in the product he is offering, incidentally. As experience demonstrates to him that Big Pharma's latest drug doesn't perform as well as the glossy brochure claimed and has killed several of his patients, the doctor's enthusiasm for the product diminishes; this is communicated by body language to the patient and the efficacy of the drug drops dramatically.

The placebo doctor is effectively hypnotising patients back to health. A silly woman investigative doctor claimed on the BBC in 2006 that healing is *only* the result of the placebo effect. It isn't. Animals can be healed and they haven't been told that healing will work. I have healed patients who didn't believe I could. What she didn't say, however, was that if the NHS prescribed, initially anyway, placebos for patients and let the Low Self do the healing you could cut the UK's drug bill by a third and also avoid the lethal side effects of many a drug. Of course, this would cut Big Pharma's profits so it's doubtful if we shall see such a policy introduced. Furthermore, if healing works as a placebo then that means you stand a 33% chance of being cured when all else has failed—so queue up for healing!

Dr Emile Coué, a turn of the 20th century physician who must have had a powerful personality, used to heal a remarkable number of his patients by getting them to recite his mantra before going to sleep. See next exercise.

Exercise 8
Dr Emile Coué's magic mantra:

'Day by day and in every way I am getting better and better.'

Not for nothing do advertisers use simple slogans. They know that the Low Self gulps them down like a dog finding a takeaway.

(a) Our minds are a bit like a washing machine.
Past the little round window will appear the mental equivalent of underwear, the sheets, the bibs and the socks in an endless display. To think people once wanted to make novels out of all this boring stuff and called it stream of consciousness fiction!

(b) Before this free association washing machine starts up recite your key thought for the day—mentally or aloud. Then, when you've got something important to think about—think about it. Another gap in your thoughts—bung in the cheering slogan.

(c) When you're going to sleep and JO is about to take over in dreams then you're closer to the Low Self. It's a good time to repeat transformational ideas such as 'Day by day and in every way I am getting better and better.'

Just keep plugging the good news.

NINE
JO the hysterical computer

The Great Organiser, sitting in front of his computer and typing in the body's health programme, is worryingly hysterical. My own JO panicked at the sight of an old-fashioned doctor's bag carried by a delightful doctor friend of mine who I had asked to read my blood pressure. I could almost hear JO whinging, 'Oh no! Oh no! Here's trouble!' (Incidentally, he was right and a problem had to be corrected.)

Perhaps JO has good reason to be frightened of doctor's as they are statistically the third largest cause of death due to medical errors and even a wrong word from a doctor can finish you off. A poor patient might have coped with a dire health situation for years until a thoughtless new doctor takes over the practice.

"Haven't you made your will yet?" He cheerily asks the sufferer.

'Oh God!' Thinks JO. 'We're cooked! I'd better LOG OFF once and for all!'

And the patient dies within a week.

On the other hand a laughing patient can send quite a different message to his or her Low Self. It seems that whole-hearted laughter will persuade the Low Self there can't be anything seriously wrong with the body and it's time to type in the 'HEALTHY' programme.

Laughter is a profound weapon in combating both physical and mental disease.

That *unihipili* has some strange quirks. It is integrated into the body and produces automatic physical responses in certain situations. For example, a dry mouth to which the tongue can stick, acquired by every soldier entering 'theatre' (i.e. a hellish combat zone) is a sign of fear. Fill the mouth with spittle, however, the reverse of the dry mouth of fear, and JO knows there's nothing to worry about and even numbs pain.

In Spain there's a Dr Angelus who uses this technique to anaesthetize patients. He attends operations where patients, their only anaesthetic a mouthful of their own spittle, have a hole drilled in their knee.

Exercise 9
Anaesthetising pain.

- (a) Get a friend to pinch you on the wrist or elsewhere if you chose. Ouch!
- (b) Fill your mouth with spittle.
- (c) Say 'My wrist is anaesthetized' mentally.
- (d) Get your friend to pinch you again and, see, you can't feel a thing!

It might come in handy some day.

TEN
Memory—Sausages in the black bag

So. Superstitious, hating criticism, a bio-computer in charge of our health, more than a little hysterical . . . what else did the Kahunas know about the *unihipili*?

They knew just how JO stores information in our memory.

We think of our memory as part of that seamless thinking whole, yet *where* is our memory? When you wish to remember the elusive name of that famous actress whose face is dancing before your mind's eye where is the memory data? Can you *see* a row of filing cabinets with one labelled, say, 'Gwyneth Paltrow', in your mind? I can't. Those who have such a natural photographic memory are a rarity.

Think of the awesome filing system needed to store all the people we know, all the useful and useless data we accumulate during our lifetimes! The Low Self is a truly marvellous librarian. In addition to storing languages, people, books we have read, memories reaching back to childhood, the Low Self also learns how to drive a car, play a guitar or operate a computer. Where is the information stored?

It's not stored on library shelves we can see and rifle through. It's stored somewhere as dark as a black bag. The 'U' of *Unihipili*, Max discovered, has the meaning of 'drawing something out of something as out of a pocket'—just as the Great Organiser will produce a memory from the dark memory store.

Well did the Kahunas call memory retrieval reaching into the black bag.

The Kahunas thought of memory as a string of sausages hidden in the black bag, a revealing analogy! Memories are associated one with the other, tied together like a string of sausages—hence the use of genomics to remember facts. Here is such a technique.

Exercise 10
A memory game

    (a)   Try and remember a shopping list: eggs, butter, bread, beans, fish, wine, DVD, bleach and you're bound to forget an item.

    (b)   However, prepare yourself with a string of memory sausage skins and you won't. The sausage skins are permanent and as long a string as you need it to be.

    (c)   Here's your sausage skin string, an impression of your movements through the house after waking up. 1. Bed, 2. Bedroom window, 3. Kitchen table, 4. Tray, 5. Teapot, 6. Stove, 7. Kettle, 8. grill . . . This is a permanent memory fixture into which you can fit anything, the more ridiculous the better.

    (d)   Put the above shopping list items in the sausage skins. Now there are eggs in your bed, butter on your bedroom window, bread on your kitchen table, beans on your tray, fish in your teapot, wine on your stove, a DVD in your kettle and bleach under the grill.

The sillier and it has to be said, the more obscene the image the easier the list is to remember.

ELEVEN
Why should The Low Self worship the Middle Self?

Now we come to the relationship of the two souls, the *unihipili* and the *uhane*. Just why should the Great Organiser slavishly worship the Clever One? As we have seen JO is the keeper of our emotions, has an awesome CCTV camera, possesses a bio-computer in charge of the body which can kill or cure you, can acquire amazing skills such as playing the piano and is in charge of our memory with all its multifarious information.

What's so special about the Middle Self soul, apart from it hogging the window of consciousness most of the time? Why does the Low Self attach itself to the Middle Self in a servant role?

The answer lies in those immensely silly dreams! During the dreaming state the Middle Self, weary with dealing with the hard realities of the physical world, has gone to sleep leaving JO in charge of consciousness. Here we observe the Great Organiser's thought patterns—and what a comically surreal jumble of reality they are—nonsense to which the dreaming Low Self gives uncritical and total credence. (And to which Freudians pay far too much credulous attention.) If the policeman in Joseph Potts BA's dream turned into a one-legged frog dancing on a pea the dreaming philosopher would still be frightened of him.

Freud, whose thinking was marred by a dictatorial streak, taking the aphorism 'if dreams were horses beggars would ride' as a guide, declared that all dreams were wish fulfilment. If a patient reported a dream of falling down a precipice and asked how this could possibly be a wish-fulfilment dream Freud would retort with Jesuitical cunning that the dreamer wished to prove Freud wrong and the dream fulfilled this wish.

Jung had a much more sensible approach to dream interpretation than Freud. Whereas Freud might declare that a dream of falling off a horse would symbolise a fear of impotence Jung would take a more pragmatic approach. Was the dreamer familiar with horses? Were they young or old? A young person might assume they would just bounce on falling off a horse whereas an old person could fear serious injury and therefore dreams with the same content might have radically different meanings for the dreamer.

Dreams, with exception of High Self precognitive dreams, are the work of a Low Self who, however brilliant it is as an organiser of bodily functions or skills, *just can't reason to save its life*. JO is totally lacking in rational skills and definitely not fit to be let loose in society. For example, left to itself that temper of Joseph Potts's Low Self would cause the philosopher to seize Mr Winkle by the throat, leading to a court appearance much more expensive outcome than the cost of the car.

Many of the old proverbs contained a shrewd understanding of the priorities of JO. 'The way to a man's heart is through his stomach' for example. This was something that a master-strategist such as Napoleon Bonaparte (not to mention many wives of the old school) knew only too well. Napoleon made sure that prisoners of the French were fed very well indeed thus imprinting on their Low Selves a love of France and a desire to sample French cuisine again as a prisoner in a future conflict.

TWELVE
ME THE ANIMAL

Are you brave enough to have an honest look at your beast below, curious reader? Remember, just as you have to know your car to repair it, you have to know your trinity of mind, especially your JO. The Kahunas sometimes knew the Low Self as the Animal Self and you might want to find out what sort of animal you are.

Writers of an earlier era often had a much more acute insight into our nature than post-Freudian writers grimly in search of the non-existent 'unconscious' mind and its equally non-existent complexes. Frank Harris, for example, is nowadays regarded as a mere hack writer but his biography of Oscar Wilde is full of superb insights, tall stories or not, and his account of Oscar's nemesis, the Marquis of Queensbury, gives us a fascinating account of that man's animal nature.

'The insane temper of the man got him into rows at the Pelican more than once,' Harris wrote. 'I remember one evening he insulted a man whom I liked immensely. Heseltine was a stockbroker, I think, a big, fair, handsome fellow who took Queensberry's insults for some time with cheerful contempt. Again and again he turned Queensberry's wrath aside with a fair word, but Queensberry went on working himself into a passion and at last made a rush at him. Heseltine watched him coming and hit out in the nick of time; he caught Queensberry full in the face and literally knocked him head over heels. Queensberry got up in a sorry mess: he had a swollen nose and black eye and his shirt was all stained with blood spread about by a hasty wiping. Any other man would have continued to fight or else have left the club on the spot; Queensberry took a seat at a table, and there sat for hours silent. I could only explain it to myself by saying that his impulse to fly at once from the scene of his disgrace was very acute and therefore he resisted it, made up his mind not to budge, and so he sat there the butt of the derisive glances and whispered talk of everyone who came into the club in the next two or three hours. He was the sort of person a wise man would avoid and a clever one would use—a dangerous, sharp, ill-handled tool.'

Does the expression 'as stubborn as a mule' come to mind regarding Queensberry? A mule being an animal with a nasty kick.

There is an image of Lakshmi, Krishna's wife, riding a tiger which indicates that her Low Self is a tiger and that her Middle Self is controlling the tiger. Are we riding the tiger or sitting on the mouse, however? It's perhaps easier to observe the Animal Self of others than perceive ones' own. We often acknowledge the animal characteristics of friends, enemies and lovers by giving them an animal name. In past times we were often much closer to our Animal Selves than we are today. In the National Portrait Gallery in London you can observe the history of the Animal Self in the faces of the English. In Tudor England almost every face has an animal content. Henry VIII, for example, with his piggy eyes, resembles nothing so much as a wild boar about to charge and gore the viewer in that brilliant Holbein portrait. Elizabeth I's spymaster Francis Walsingham is a fox. The Animal Self stares nakedly from the faces of these people—with the exception of Elizabeth herself who presents a doll-like mask to the world.

As society standardises education, and becomes more and more restrictive of our basic urges and cushions the grim realities of life, however, the animal gradually diminishes, with a few exceptions, from the face of England until we end with the bespectacled pudding of the 20th century intellectual. When Ford Madox Ford first encountered DH Lawrence in his editorial offices, however, he described in his memoirs how a little red-bearded fox walked in so a few Animal Selves were still out and about.

How do we discover our inmost animal nature? One way is to be attacked in the street. I was once attacked and discovered that I was, in fact, a bear capable of lifting a fellow as heavy as myself up and slamming him against a bus. My JO, after a lifetime's caution, hugely enjoyed his violent outing and the incident gave me a valuable insight into the causes of street violence.

There's a strain of thought in modern life which demonises the animal. "They behaved like animals," we say self-righteously in describing all too human behaviour. Now while animals have some unsavoury habits (as well as being capable of great devotion) none of them launch such mighty attacks, aided and abetted by the latest gadget provided by white-coated devils, upon their own species as we rational human beings habitually do in the 'theatre' of war. How about 'They behaved like humans' as a term of abuse?

Spiritual development can be a paradoxical business. It's frequently said that we must suppress the animal within ourselves to develop spiritually. This is a disastrous mistake. As we shall see, if we are to reach the High Self it is the energy provided by the Low Self, the Animal Self *that enables us to make contact!* To suppress our JO in order to develop spiritually is like shooting one's horse before setting out on a long journey. It's totally self-defeating.

To the ancients there was no barrier between the human and animal soul. There were all fashioned from the same spiritual substance and hence could be intermingled. The sphinx combines the power of the lion with the rational power of the human head. The 'Winged Bull', guardian of the temple of Nineveh, which gives the title to Dion Fortune's novel of the same name, combines the strength and virility of the bull with the wings of the divine and the reasoning power of the human. Only if you take an 'us and them' attitude to our spiritual substance, whereby animals belong to a different and contemptibly lower order of being, does the sphinx become an inexplicable phenomenon.

The white-coated scientific devil, projecting his mechanistic and psychotic view of the world, makes the astonishing claim that animals have no feelings. As anyone who has owned a dog will realise, only a madman would claim that animals don't feel hunger, pain, pleasure or stress. The distressing modern practice of crating your dog has grown from this scientific misunderstanding. More than feeling pain or pleasure, however, dogs are capable of a whole range of emotions and attitudes. Dogs can fall in love, be good or bad parents, suffer from ego problems and fear losing face. In fact, their mind games are remarkably similar to our own.

Animals—apart from the angry bear chasing one through the wilds or the crocodile leaping out of the swamp—are, far from being the antithesis of our spirituality, an essential part of it. Our Low Self receives spiritual nourishment from the company of an animal. Stroking a pet will even help your health by enabling you to finely tune our bio-computer to those peaceful, immemorial, animal rhythms.

As for personal animal characteristics, remember that whatever the character of your JO, for good or ill you are stuck with that character. It's no use trying to turn a mouse into a tiger or carthorse into a bear. You don't want to get into a conflict on the assumption you're a deadly tiger and find you're a mouse half way through, do you? It could be difficult.

Exercise 10
Discovering your Animal Self

Self-knowledge is painful to acquire but immensely valuable when you have it and knowledge of your animal self is an important place to start. Of course, when we judge ourselves we are extremely partial and likely to come up with a 'not guilty' verdict.

(a) Choose the animal that you consider is like yourself in important ways.
(b) Get a friend to choose which animal represents you.
(c) Don't be annoyed with your friend but consider which of the animals is nearest to your character.

THIRTEEN
GETTING TO KNOW JO

More aware reader, you should now be getting a feeling for your Unihipili, a feeling of knowing intellectually what you've already known intuitively perhaps. Could it be that you feel that at last you're acknowledging the neglected helper, the faithful inner child, and devoted slave who you've sometimes abused? Now is the time to get to know the real you—a very important process if you want to lead your own happy life and don't want the likes of Derren Brown, Tony Friendly or anyone else for that matter, plugging into your JO for their own nefarious purposes.

To some extent getting to know our inner child is a question of honest introspection for, throbbing away within us, almost within grasp, is the emotional nexus of JO. This is the character who mislays the Greenpeace envelope and makes dedicated vegetarians stuff themselves on hog roast at a barbecue.

If you occasionally drink far too much you might be unlucky enough to have a blackout which is where the tape recorder in the brain is switched off by alcohol. In the morning, apart from a raging hangover, there is a worrying sense that beyond eight-thirty there's only a big blank hole in the memory where the rest of the evening should be and try as you may you can't remember a thing. It's quite possible that your JO has escaped during those lost hours. If you're a man hope the bodies aren't found; if you're a woman you were probably dancing naked on a table somewhere and it's advisable to take the Morning After Pill.

Who are your favourite icons? These people walk our walk, sing our song, dance our dance, embody what our Low Self really, really, really would like to do given the chance. Perhaps like Lady Diana they embody our High Self aspirations. Alas, even our higher aspirations are not without danger as we're just as likely to be taken in by the spiritual swindler as the crook selling time-shares. 'Break free from material ties, spiritual student, and put your property in my name,' says Swami Reeleevjo Hovyamoni.

Perhaps it's relatively harmless that you're rooting for Tony Soprano instead of joining the Tosho Enlightenment Society.

Your JO would just love to be able to waste your hated enemies like stressed-out Big Tony with the smoking, hooded eyes instead of leading a suppressed, timid, suburban existence. But it's only entertainment. Tony Soprano is an unusual gangster figure as he represents a violent Low Self who might have the satisfaction of killing a colleague in a rage and yet is subject to the constraints of the mafia job and the encircling FBI and needs Middle Self cunning to survive. He also suffers frim fainting attacks. Most screen gangsters are just rampaging JOs which is why we love them so much as they represent Low Self freedom, a freedom which we haven't enjoyed since childhood.

Suggestibility. How suggestible are you? Do you just go with the flow? When your doctor says, 'Take this' do you just take it? Do you have strong beliefs and get very agitated if challenged? Do you belong to a political party which is going to save the world? Are you frightened of attracting the attention of shop assistants because you won't be able to refuse buying something once they've taken charge of you? Do you possess several objects which you didn't intend to buy and now wish you hadn't? Do stage magicians invite you to become part of their act? If the answer to some or most of these questions is 'Yes' then you are suggestible.

Takes one to know one. What faults do you hate in others? Alas, it takes one to know one. When we look at the world of people or things we are looking into a mirror for if it doesn't exist within us then we can't see it without us. 'Oh! That woman is such a cunning minx!' Indeed she is, and only your own cunning enables you to perceive it. Incidentally, there's nothing wrong with a bit of cunning which is necessary for our survival and success. Cunning is like magic, black or white according to the purposes to which it is put.

"I can't stand that fellow," I hear you say. "He talks about nothing but himself." Hmm? Indeed he does but have you ever listened to yourself rambling on?

On the other hand do you know a person who is genuinely in touch with their High Self, the sort who always seems to be happy without much money and gets a lot out of nature and meditation and talks about strange spiritual experiences?

These oddballs don't seem to recognise just how nasty people can be.

"Isn't X a disgusting miser?" you say. "He's got loads of money and he won't even pay the builders after they've done the work."

"It's only because his mother took his puppy away when he was four," says the sainted one. "X is all right."

Greed isn't in them and they can't see it in others.

Are you brave enough to find out from your friends what they really think of you? Remember, they're still your friends despite those madly irritating traits of yours which you only notice in other people. In fact, your friends, observing only what's to be seen of your behaviour and excluded from your intimate thought processes (which you think comprises the real you and which you wouldn't share with anyone) probably know more about your JO than you do. Similarly, pre-Freudian writers such as Frank Harris, describing their subject in terms of animal traits, ambition, determination, cowardice etc, often provide a better description of their subject than far-fetched, sexually obsessed psychoanalysts piddling about in the unconscious mind. Of course, now that vaginal, anal and oral sex, not to mention other human strange indulgences, are a common feature of TV the psychoanalytic obsession with such matters seems more than a tad old-fashioned.

How masculine or feminine are you? The male and female Low Selves differ in many respects from each other, though how much this is to due to social conditioning it's sometimes difficult to say. Women seem to enjoy flying aircraft or doing factory work when given the opportunity. Nature versus Nurture? Scientifically it has been observed that women are more academic that men and better at performing delicate tasks. Women are much more open to psychic matters and intuitive feelings than most men. Women also tend to be much earthier than men, more in touch with their basic emotions and more aware of the psychology of relationships.

Men have a tendency to go on automatic pilot, possibly the result of anticipating a lengthy career (though this is no longer the case in the UK.). In a war situation the female JO wants to reproduce while the male wants to kill. However, put a woman like Mrs Thatcher in charge of society, and she will make war much more happily than a general who has actually experienced its horrors. The Low Selves of the UK voters, incidentally, confused killing foreigners with national self-interest and eagerly voted Mrs T back into power after she engaged in the Falklands War. I'm delighted to say that the soul of the UK has matured over the years and the mass protests concerning the Iraq war indicated that the British public has realised at last that war is not a natural, moral or profitable national game.

There's no such thing as the purely aggressive male JO or a purely nurturing female one. We have subtle blends of sexuality, subtle blends of nurture and violence and, whatever our sexuality, violent emotions frequently crowd up upon us from the Low Self. In a mother's case murderous but helpless rage might be directed against the filthy minx who has got her sex claws into Beloved Perfect Son. But poor Mum has to bite her tongue and pretend to like the damned woman while dreaming that she's a friend of Tony Soprano who will kill the bitch as a favour.

Some men are more motherly than mothers. I myself enjoyed the role of househusband when my girls weren't driving me round the bend. Some women have no sense of motherhood and just dump their children and run. Recognise your complex sexual agendas. It will help you deal with them.

More aware reader, the character of your Unihipili, Low Self, your JO should be more within your grasp. Here is the Great Organiser, in charge of your memory, driving your car, armed with a CCTV camera that records all your experience, fearing God and desperate to WINWINWIN. Yet this brilliant bio-computer just can't think straight, is sometimes lost in surreal confusion and is easy prey for the manipulator, be it personal, political or commercial.

In fact—and this is extremely important if you wish to be happy—THE LOW SELF FINDS IT DIFFICULT TO DISTINGUISH BETWEEN FACT AND FANTASY.

This is all too apparent in Low Self people who believe soap characters are real and that Sherlock Homes really does live in Baker Street. The confusion of a humble viewer is understandable enough. What is more bizarre is the way the media will use a movie to inspire a political debate about real events. The Low Self interest dominates the media with its obsession with sports, sex and success.

FOURTEEN
THE MIDDLE SELF
THE UHANE
MYSELF THE CLEVER ONE

When the mind says, 'Walk' the body walks.
Frederick the Great
Aye but thought's the slave of life
Shakespeare

So which soul does JO slave for during a lifetime?

It's us up here, the Middle Self, the bit of us hogging the window of consciousness and reading this, the rational part of us which we can easily mistake, due to the smooth interaction of the trinity of mind, for our entire soul. A university degree with consequent intellectual arrogance can seal this delusion for life. Modern education can also be an effective method of preventing thought.

JO desperately needs the guidance of the Middle Self. We can see in the surreal nonsense of dreams or the ghastly muddled panic created when the Low Self takes over our lives after a nervous breakdown that poor JO, the bio-computer of genius, is sadly lacking when it comes to rational thought. The thought patterns of JO are not dissimilar to those of one's dog. I once had a dog called Spike who tried out his teeth on an electric fence and had to be lifted over all fences thereafter, convinced that they would set his teeth on fire. That's Low Self thinking and illustrates why the great Organiser looks up to the Clever One and is such an obedient servant. The Low Self is in awe of the Middle Self's reasoning ability.

When we awake from dream nonsense the Low Self has to cope with a real physical world where you will *not* wake up in your bed or turn into a clothes hanger after being run over by a double-decker bus. There is a remorseless logic about the physical world which is at odds with the all-embracing desires of JO. The Middle Self has to put on the harness and saddle of reality to guide JO through the dangerous jungle of everyday life.

Take smoking, for example. It tastes horrible at first but then the Middle Self becomes a fashion victim. Those fags look so cool in public, don't they? Movies stars, not to mention the likes of gangsters, use them. The *image* of smoking, rather than the foul-tasting reality, is imposed upon the reluctant Low Self. Even the SMOKING KILLS warning becomes part of the cool, death-defying, post-modern experience. An addicted JO will choke on the smoke until dropping dead in an oxygen tent.

To avoid such an unhappy outcome the Clever One has to take charge, pointing out the danger of oral and lung cancers, the expense, the harm to secondary smokers, the bad breath and the sheer aridity of the smoking experience. Smoking doesn't actually calm you down at all. It doesn't cheer you up like booze. It does nothing for you at all but create the need for yet another fag. It is a foul-smelling addiction for the sake of addiction. It is bad news. The Middle Self, having rationally chosen to stop smoking, has to apply *will* to stop the obnoxious habit. NOW.

The Low Self, the younger brother or sister, desperately needs the guidance of the older and wiser Middle Self in such matters.

JO, so sadly lacking in self-restraint, would get us kicked onto the fringes of society if let out and about and needs the guidance of Myself in the difficult business of life generally.

Only the Uhane can make the big decisions of life. What if you're stuck in the wrong job and should give up being manager of the supermarket and try for a career in journalism? What if your husband is too controlling and is restricting your personality and career possibilities?

Robot JO will soldier on in all circumstances. Only the Middle Self can take the overview. There is a conflict between the agenda of the two. Robot JO will just go on and on and on despite horrific circumstances. Most people would die rather than think, declared Bertrand Russell. Thinking is therefore dangerous for cultures or an unsatisfactory way of life—which is why people are frightened of thinking.

But if we're going to think we have to think clearly and hence we owe it to ourselves to hone our rational skills.

What is rational, however? As far as I am concerned being rational includes recognition of the value of intuition. Intuition is information garnered from the High Self rather than that perceived by the rational Middle Self.

That control freak of a husband, for example. When you first met him you experienced a pang in the solar plexus; your High Self had perceived that, despite his soft words, there was a domineering side to his character, which didn't go with his professed New Age beliefs and the marriage was going to be a disaster. In the registry office you felt really depressed as you were spliced. Intuitively you knew this was a mistake but your Middle Self refused to recognise it. Now you need to get sliced!

Or supposing two properties appeal to a couple; one property a bit run down but which the girl senses has a good atmosphere. The other needs no work but has a dreadful atmosphere. While Mister would like to spare the DIY and go for the smart house I would advise investigating the bad atmosphere. It could be from a transformer nearby or a Hellphone mast or bad energies coming up through the earth. Some of these can prove lethal to your health or at best make life very depressing.

In fact, psychically aware people aren't silly or precious. They're smart and well worth listening to.

An ounce of real intuition can be worth a ton of laborious thought. In some cases, however, we need to be able to investigate and weigh the evidence—as to how far that career in journalism is possible, for example.

Modern life is full of complex issues such as, 'Will nuclear power save the planet?' (No!) We need to be able to get our head round the evidence if we are to have any influence at all on the world at large. If enough people in the world thought rationally about their real self-interest we would live in a very different world from the one that exists at the moment. We owe it to ourselves to sift the evidence, sort the lies out from the truth and come to a reasonable conclusion about personal and social issues.

Apart from reason the other great power of the Middle Self is: *CHOICE!!!!*

The Middle Self has vast power over JO and can lead the Great Organiser into a war zone, into an exploitative religious cult, into a disastrous marriage, into a dead-end career or a fulfilled life. The Uhane therefore has a huge responsibility for the life an individual chooses to lead.

Yet sometimes life just seems to happen to us. Sometimes we just seem fated to have the life we have. Perhaps we don't like our job or our marriage particularly. Family responsibilities and society consign us to that boring job in the supermarket or whatever.

"Our fates are foreshapen, roughhew them how we may," as Shakespeare put it. Fatalism. The great social octopus has us within its tentacles and there's nothing much we can do about it.

Suppose, through having to pay the mortgage and feed the children, we are really and truly stuck in our rut and there's no way out.

The Middle Self then has *THE GREAT CHOICE OF HOW WE FEEL!!!*

The same circumstances can look very different depending on how we construe them. Is the glass half full or half empty? This is a crucial choice as we shall see.

Reason, choice and . . .

The other great power of Myself is the power of WILL.

D.H. Lawrence hated the mechanical aspect of will (while being extremely wilful himself) and wrote a series of brilliant stories about nasty wilful people who'd willed their child into a psychological corner but then got their comeuppance. He saw the mechanical will as a negation of the natural ebb and flow of the life force, an enemy of life itself.

Is will good or bad, however?

Actually, it all depends what will is applied to. If Lorenzo had given up writing after nasty reviews and censorship of his novel we'd have lost invaluable literature. His will kept him going. If you will yourself to carry your project through and you make a million then you can say, "I've got the willpower to succeed." If you end up in debt after ten years of wasted effort then you can only conclude, "I've got the willpower to waste ten years of my life."

Will is sometimes needed with psychic matters. If you want to become a clairvoyant and aren't naturally gifted you might have to stare at a crystal ball for hours a day for years until a connection with higher powers is made.

If will is put to a bad cause then it's bad. No one's going to applaud the dedication and willpower of a serial killer, for example.

We all need some of the stuff, however. Have you ever met people who seem to have no will whatever and get blown this way and that by every influence like mental thistledown? It won't do. We need the willpower to hang on to a positive idea.

Reason, choice and will, the three assets of the Middle Self.

You might think that as Joseph Potts B.A. I would rate intellectual people way above JO People and think the clever academic ones are a superior sort of secular saint. It ain't necessarily so.

Whereas the JO person is likely to have open eyes and a mobile expression, the deadpan features of the Middle Self person can appear positively insectoid. A JO person is likely to become noisy and aggressive if you contradict a favourite belief but Middle Self, intellectually conceited people will just stare through their bifocals with cold contempt. Rather than a brawl in the pub garden, the 'educated' Clever One will have a battle of wills over the best means of flying a kite or baking a loaf of soda bread or blowing up the world.

Nothing in excess, as the Delphic Oracle says.

The problem is that over-educated Middle Self people can become prisoner of their so-called expertise. Their education has just papered the mental prison walls with their degrees. No person trained in Freudian psychiatry or drug treatment for mental problems would take this book seriously for a single moment, for example. Neither would a modern physicist take the discoveries of Viktor Schauberger seriously for a single moment either, despite the fact that his flumes could float heavier than water timber for miles and the Austrian government paid him in gold because of inflation of the Mark.

Is an expert someone who has made a career out of being wrong?

In every aspect of our lives there is an expert claiming supreme knowledge. These experts 'knew' those apparently respectable, caring middle-class parents had really murdered their babies, that 'weeds' must be expensively removed from pasture even if cattle will thrive on these same 'weeds', that nature can be genetically reprogrammed for our benefit, that we need fluoride (a substance only slighter less poisonous than lead) dunked in our water supply while medical experts are sometimes happy to prescribe expensive drugs which only treat but never cure a health problem when a change of diet would do the trick.

And what's happened to the Low Self of the expert? Although your average scientist may look as far removed from a noisy binge drinker as possible as he gives that Praying Mantis stare through his bifocals, alas, behind that white coat they throbs a JO not dissimilar to that of the drunk on the streets.

The Kahuna Kit

The scientists of the Manhattan Project who exploded the first atom bomb half-expected their atomic explosion to set off a chain reaction which would eat up the entire planet. They pressed the button anyway. Why? Testosterone? Ambition? Scientific curiosity? Whatever the motive was it clearly overcame any sense of responsibility to Planet Earth. Heck, if they screwed the poodle there was going to be no one around to call them to account anyway!

Unfortunately this is far from an isolated incident and white-coated devils are engaging in horrendous, planet-endangering experiments to this day. It's astonishing that we're all still here and it's perfectly possible that one day some bug-eyed scientific nerd will press the wrong button and baboombaboombaboom! A perfect illustration of this is the Cern particle accelerator. This wasteful project is built underground—which clearly indicates that the white-coated devils fear an explosion of some sort. The very terms of the billion pound project are that they don't know what they're doing as they crash energy particles together, hopefully generating the heat of creation and searching among the electronic debris for the 'God particle' which caused the Big Bang. Interestingly enough, Olaf Thomas Rabbe argues convincingly in the October-November edition of 'Nexus' magazine that these lethal nerds at Cern are the cause of a series of mysterious nuclear-type explosions in the atmosphere. In their search for notoriety and Nobel Prizes—for, as we have seen, Low Self greed lurks beneath the white coat—these bug-eyed nonentities inspired by fireworks night might well have created a series of mini black holes.

It is a prime example how the religion of mechanistic science (whose papal spokesman at the moment is Dawkins) has so polluted our society that it seems entirely proper to put the earth itself at risk to satisfy the sacred pursuit of scientific curiosity.

Here is the voice of a real scientist.

'I do not know how I appear to the world,' wrote Sir Isaac Newton. 'But to myself I seem to have been a boy playing on the seashore and diverting myself, now and then finding a smoother pebble or a prettier shell than ordinary, whilst the great ocean of truth lay all undiscovered before me.' Newton was as preoccupied with psychic science as he was with mechanical science and the more he learned the more he realised there was to learn. The know-all, white-coated devil, however, the mechanist who claims we have no minds, will claim to know every atom of every pebble on every beach in every universe by name.

We desperately need men of integrity in science. Open-minded and honest scientists are exciting people. The blinkered hirelings of dark forces are a frightening phenomena, however, and illustrate how easily the Middle Self can be led astray.

Clarity of thought is both a practical necessity and spiritual duty.

FIFTEEN
SMARTEN UP!
A child's guide to philosophy

'Philosophy is simply the grammar of a language made extant'
Nietzsche

Bertrand Russell often maintained that people would rather die than think and if you don't like thought you'd better bunk this item! It's designed to help your Middle Self by acquainting you with some of the basics of that deeply disturbing and subversive subject—philosophy. Incidentally, none other authority than Aleister Crowley recommended a study of philosophy to be a useful starter for the study of Magick.

We tend to think of spiritual development only in terms of the High Self, drawing closer to the God Within. It's all higher-vibrational stuff merging with the ether.

However, the Middle Self is also a soul which needs development and help just as much as the Low Self and the High Self.

The Buddhists regard stupidity as a spiritual crime.

And what a huge sea change there would be in human affairs, what an historical parting of the ways, *if we humans simply thought calmly and clearly about where our true interests lay.*

To improve human affairs enormously we don't need to access higher spiritual powers!

We simply need to think clearly!

Improving clarity of thought of the Middle Self is a very different matter than relating to the Low Self or the High Self. As we have seen the Low Self regards all criticism, criticism of anything at all, no matter how worthy a target, as a blot on the psychic landscape. Similarly, as we shall see, in the world of the High Self *there are no negatives.* There is no division and therefore no comparison. Bewilderingly the High Self is beyond the reach of philosophy, altogether beyond logic. The Low Self might well have caught a dislike of criticism from its secret relationship with the High Self where division doesn't exist.

The Middle Self, however, is grappling with the physical world which is laden with dangers and complicated choices! What sort of mortgage? What car? Shall I have the kids vaccinated? This world contains negatives in abundance and clarity of thought and informed choice is essential for financial and, in the case of medical issues, perhaps physical survival.

Let me give you some examples of the dangers of sloppy thinking. In the beginning was the word! Now it might seem that today in the age of the flashing, singing and mind-grabbing video that the word is a bit outmoded. Yet the word still dominates our behaviour and thought.

One of the first rules of philosophy is to analyse your terms, your words. If there is a flaw in understanding your terms then no valid thinking can develop. You're stuffed before you start.

Don't just take that word of trust. Find out what it means.

SEXISM. Oooh! Terrible! Rape! Treating women as sex objects instead of people! Male chauvinism! Women in a horrible legal disadvantage in marriage! Not treating women the same as men! Shocking! Not treating women as human beings! Pornography!

But let's look closely at the implications of the above.

'Treating women as sex objects' for starters. The problem with this cliché is that from adolescence onwards Mother Nature has charged us up with enormously powerful sex urges to make sure the human race continues to exist and the younger we are and the more likely we are to breed, the more our perception of the opposite sex, (not to mention those of same sex attraction) is the perception of sex objects! 'Cor!' thinks the calf male. 'What a pair of knockers!' And though he is delighted she likes music as well and can sing in his band it's *her as sex object* that drew him to her side initially. Perhaps, in the fullness of time, like Annie Lennox and Dave Stewart, their musical partnership became more important than the initial sexual attraction but sex was the original magnet. Greta Garbo, Paulette Goddard, Marlene Dietrich, Marilyn Monroe, Veronica Lake, Gwyneth Paltrow—it wasn't their intellectual powers (even though some of them were very clever women and brilliant actresses) that burnt them into the mass psyche, was it now?

It's becoming more and more apparent as sexual attitudes are liberated that women—surprise, surprise—are equally capable of viewing men as 'mere' sex objects and observing, for example, 'Phew! He's well hung! Nice bum too.' Movie beefcake has, in fact, long enshrined the male as sex object for women moviegoers. As a man I can say that being regarded (favourably) as a sex object is cheering rather than degrading.

Of course, as life sometimes brutally teaches us, there's much more to relationships than sex objects banging each other but, if it weren't for sexual attraction based on sexual characteristics in the first place the human race would rapidly cease to exist. Oh, let's stop pretending! There are books analysing sexual characteristics—even the most attractive facial proportions are known—and their powerful attraction for the opposite sex. Psychologists and admen know all about it! Yes, women and men, like it or not, if they're sexually active are sex objects for each other!

It's equally obvious that men and women have other relationships apart from sexual ones—parental relationships or professional relationships or intellectual relationships—and, as we age and desires wane, we begin to perceive members of the opposite sex as friends or professionals—though sex always lurks in the background and a sexual thought is apparently one of our last.

What about 'not treating women the same as men'? Again there's a problem with this one. Women are *not* the same as men. For a start girls are academically smarter than boys and for years were unfairly hobbled within the English educational system to keep them back and stop them giving boys an inferiority complex!

Anyone who's had children will have noticed the difference between the testosterone-driven, 'Here I am!' small boy and the much more mature girl who quietly gets on with her interests.

What about sexual harassment? Well, it's a pain to be hit on by someone you don't fancy, just as it's delightful to be hit on by someone you do fancy.

"Two quid to you, darling," says the barrow boy.

"I'm not your darling," snarls the feminist. But isn't—or rather wasn't—the 'darling' word an expression an old-fashioned male chivalry? Weren't most men once rather instinctively kind to women before feminism took hold?

And now that men instead of women are at a horrible legal disadvantage in marriage we might all, women included, consider whether this is such a good thing. Society is full of unintended consequences. Might it not have resulted in so many young professional men, terrified of being kicked out of the family home like dad, living apart instead of finding a wife and committing themselves to the perilous business of raising a family and hasn't this placed a strain on the housing market in the UK? Hasn't feminism driven a wedge between the sexes? Hasn't feminism caused the break up of many a family unit?

So this word 'sexism' looks a bit flaky when we examine it. It condemns the very force, sexual attraction, that keeps the human race in existence, denies the very real differences that exist between men and women, divides the sexes and yet it is used as if it is a triumphant and unassailable philosophy.

Take another 'ism'—racism. RACISM! Horrible! Terrible! Pogroms! Massacres! Condemning a person because of their colour!

But what does 'racism' actually *mean*? Killing people of a foreign race, disadvantaging people of a foreign race, thinking that you belong to a superior race, abusing people of a foreign race, making reasonable criticisms of people of a foreign race, bonding to 'your own' country and culture, or preferring the company of your own race?

I think we can all agree that killing people of foreign race, just because they're foreign, is a bad practice. Underlying the Iraq war was a genuinely racist assumption that what happened to the Iraqis didn't matter, that a terrifying bombardment from the air, unthinkable if smashing the infrastructure of London or New York, was acceptable because it was inflicted on a foreign race and alien culture.

Furthermore, a smug assumption of racial superiority is likely to result in nasty shocks. Hitler attacked the Russians assuming that they were racial inferiors but the inferior race, with a little help from the Russian winter, destroyed him. Once the Englishman was encouraged to regard himself as a member of a master race, though the English, invaded by Vikings, Romans, Normans and breeding with many immigrants are not really a race at all. If we in the West still regard ourselves as a superior race we will discover with the development of China and India just how good these 'inferiors' are at business and science and sport. An assumption of racial superiority is not limited to westerners, however. Chinese, Japanese and Muslims, for example, are just as likely to regard other races with contempt.

And is it such a terrible thing to bond to your own country and culture? Is there such as thing as 'my country'? Well, surely the Chinese have some right to China, the Africans to Africa, the Indians to India and even the mongrel British to the UK! To turf all the Chinese out of China and send

Africans to live there would seem to me to be morally wrong—not to mention an impossible goal given the strength of the Chinese People's Army and Chinese military technology. It seems to me that there is a sense in which 'my country' is a perfectly valid concept. Otherwise the world could consist of nothing but displaced persons.

Is preferring the company of your own race racist? If it is then every immigrant group in the UK which has formed itself into a tight ethnic community must be considered racist. In Dorset (the county in the South of the UK where I live) in the not so distant past villagers used to regard those even in the next village as foreigners and a girl who married someone from a different village was considered a traitor and might even be physically attacked. To prefer the company of your own sort therefore may not be very enlightened but it is, alas, all-too-human.

The word 'racism' is beginning to look like a 'wouldn't-it-be-nice' concept rather than a sound moral declaration.

As for disadvantaging people of a different race . . . well, as Brits in Spain or Goa who've bought properties and find them suddenly rendered worthless by planning regulations are discovering . . . this is what happens to foreigners. They get disadvantaged. It's the way of world.

Is justly criticising foreigners racist? Well, just because someone's a foreigner it doesn't mean they've been parachuted in from heaven! If we can't criticise foreigners then we're according them a bizarre special status! Surely rational criticism of any group is perfectly justified.

So here we have two words, sexism and racism, two triumphant agendas with legal implications which shape our society and yet which fly in the face of basic human nature when we look at them closely. One condemns the sexuality which keeps the human race going while the other condemns the geographical and cultural bonding which, reprehensible or not, is an essential part of the human experience.

These words which so dominate our society are at best pious *hopes* for the future of an enlightened mankind!

Here we see the dangers of words which become inserts to control our behaviour.

Handle language as if words were tarantulas.

Words can come with an inbuilt emotional load which colour the same facts differently.

'Tony Blair made the *tough* decision to go to war with Iraq.'

'Tony Blair made the *brutal* decision to go to war with Iraq.'

Both words refer to the same facts.

Sometimes words, manipulated by social forces, can take on a weird, positively alchemical, life of their own.

Take the word 'art' which originally meant nothing more than 'fitting'—originating from the Latin '*ars*'—so that a statue of Zeus might be fitting for a Roman Temple, for example. Much later the word acquired a portentous value and certain activities such as painting and sculpture and classical music became classed as 'artistic activities'.

However, the mere act of framing a painting doesn't make it a work of art. If you can't paint and you frame and display your rubbish you haven't created a work of art you've just made a bit of a fool of yourself—though if you're enjoying yourself who cares?

Certain artists created impossibly great objects. Greek sculpture looks as if a god rather than a human carved it. Rembrandt creates some portraits which stare back at one from the canvas as if they are alive. The success of sculpture, painting and classical music meant that critics, those non-creative, self-appointed guardians of quality, denied that any other activity could be an art. After sculpture and painting and classical music they placed a big final full stop.

When Jazz burst on stage in the 20th century critics declared it couldn't possibly be an art because ignorant black people who had never been to music conservatory created it. In fact, jazz became *the* musical modern art of the 20th century and great composer Stravinsky on arrival in America dashed off to the Cotton Club to hear Duke Ellington. Art snobbery prevented many iconic poets of sound such as Charlie Parker or Ben Webster enjoying their due recognition and celebration. Duke Ellington, for my money the 20th century's greatest composer, was savaged by the IRS late in his career as if he were nothing but a common swindler and made to surrender the copyrights of his life's work. "All I have is my dreams," he said.

In fact, art means simply '*that which is great.*' If we have a great meal we say 'that meal was a work of art.' One of the most touching and wonderful things about us humans is that we can take any activity whatever and by an extraordinary dedication and genius we can raise it to the level of art. Art is that which is great.

Of course, infants would vote for the Teletubbies over Goya if asked to judge art. Yeah, but they're infants. If you insist on grading art you would grade it in terms of its *audience* rather than searching for some quite illusory ultimate values. There aren't any ultimate values by which you can measure art or even decide what is and isn't art. Some black kid tap-dancing on a street corner may be more of an artist than an RA who has created a highly finished but lifeless oil painting. The greatest art critic of all times was John Ruskin who became a geologist and meteorologist and skilled artist to understand the works of Turner. Ruskin in his declining years then damned a painting by Whistler, accusing him of being a coxcomb who had thrown a pot of paint in the public's face, when Whistler was using some of the same impressionistic techniques as Turner himself. If Ruskin couldn't get it right then no art critic can get it right. Teletubbies for infants, Damien Worst for fashion victims, Blake for mystics, Matisse for colourists and so on. Your mystic audience who understood Blake would make a useful group to examine the work of a contemporary mystic painter whereas it would be no use asking the infants or fashion victims for their opinion.

Unfortunately, the word 'art' has now become traded as a word which can achieve absurd miracles of alchemy. Attach the word 'art' to anything under the sun—urinals, bricks, self-mutilation, pickled sheep, rubbish, tinned pooh, people running to and fro or light bulbs going on an off—and apparently, just as the pumpkin was transformed into Cinderella's carriage, it becomes ART.

In fact, if everything is art then nothing is art. In an all black world there would be no word for black, because, if there were no white, we would be unable to distinguish black from white. If everything under the sun is art then there's no non-art and therefore no word for art.

The urinals, bricks, self-mutilation, pickled sheep, rubbish, tinned pooh, people running to and fro or lights being turned on an off remain exactly what they are—urinals, bricks, self-mutilation, pickled sheep, rubbish, tinned pooh, people running to and fro or lights being turned on and off. The fact that a considerable number of fashion victims remain convinced otherwise shows *the frightening power of words.*

Imagine going to a restaurant and being fed lead shot instead of caviar.

"Waiter! I can't eat this. This is lead shot."

"That's irrelevant, sir. Eat up. This is a restaurant and whatever is in a restaurant is food."

At a more sombre level words lead us to war. We in the UK have had a recent experience of how we were led into war by Tony Blair on the basis of a lie—namely that Saddam Hussein possessed weapons of mass destruction. A process of demonization of a person or a race generally precedes a war and, once we hear that increasingly tired sentence 'He is like Hitler', then we can guarantee that war is at hand.

Note that in war we enter, is not the slaughterhouse of war, but the 'theatre of war' rather like an operating theatre or an evening at the theatre . . . to watch a tragedy or the theatre of cruelty, perhaps. Just imagine that war was described as the 'slaughterhouse' instead of 'theatre' and politicians and military men had to report, 'Yes, our men have been in slaughterhouse for two months now . . .'

The war-mongering politician is adept at luring the Low Self into war. The Low Self is healthily aggressive to protect its assets and family and the war-monger plays on this healthy enough instinct by persuading us that the bloodthirsty Xs will eat babies, rape wives and put a match to the homestead just as Saddam was supposed to be able to blast the UK within 45 minutes.

A war to defend ourselves against a cruel foreign race who would enslave us seems to be a sound enough idea but the UK has hardly ever engaged in a war of this nature—ever since the Normans invaded us and did just that.

Words—still deadly despite the wonders of film and music.

Words—slippery as greased rattlesnakes!

If we can't trust words what can we know for certain?

Philosophers have long been preoccupied by the question: "How do we know anything for sure?" Despite their finest efforts, their creation of systems of knowledge based upon some apparently ultimate truth, the final answer when all the philosophical dust has settled is a disappointing one.

Watching some physicist nerd scrawl incomprehensible equations on the blackboard we groundlings think, 'That must be real. That's how they created the atomic bomb.' But does maths have a rational basis?

Bertrand Russell was preoccupied with finding a logical basis for mathematics, spent many years on the task, nearly drove himself to a nervous breakdown and was paid £35 for writing 'Principia Mathematica'. Although it made his reputation it is a flawed work and doesn't give maths a logical basis.

In the succeeding decades maths fanatics have literally driven themselves into insanity in the quest to give maths a logical basis—without any success. Does 1+1=2 in the same way that 2=2, for example? If 1+1 is conceptually or logically different from 2 then it clearly doesn't equal 2. 1+1=1+1. In the abstract world how exactly are 1+1 separate as opposed to being conjoined in 2? Is 1 a millimetre or a kilometre apart from 1 in 1+1?

Of course, in the real physical world 1+1 doesn't necessarily equal 2 at all. One plus one mice of opposite sex can equal hundreds of mice given time. One rotten apple and one good apple together equals no apples while in the world of quantum experiments 2 beams of light can equal 3 beams of light. Maths just hasn't a logical basis. You can't get any more out of the logical pot then you put in. What is, is! And that's it!

If we want to sum up the final conclusion of modern philosophy it could be:

'We know nothing at all about anything despite our best efforts.'

Philosophers delight in destroying our most cherished beliefs. For example, they point out gleefully, just because the sun has risen in the past that's no guarantee that it will rise in the future. After all a chicken might reason that it would be fed on Christmas Eve as it has been fed all year. And the past doesn't guarantee the future at all. Certainly in social terms this is only too true. The baby boomer generation have seen bizarre upheavals in society from the utopian promise of the sixties, through unnecessary wars, social attitudes being stood on their head and now the financial downturns of the present whereby apparently rock-solid financial institutions melt before our eyes.

So what is logical? In society we find if we live long enough that values are stood on their head. Can we even rely upon the earth itself which religious nuts of physicists feel entitled to blow up in their Jesuitical search for truth? Perhaps at least logic will provide us with something utterly reliable.

I was very disappointed by logic when I first learnt about it. It seemed painfully limited to what was blazingly obvious. Take the syllogism, for example:

All men die
Tony Blair is a man
Tony Blair will die

Joe Potts

Yawn! Yawn! Hardly groundbreaking stuff is it?

All fish swim in the sea
Whales swim in the sea
Whales are fish

Wrong. Fooled yah! Whales are mammals but, like men, swim in the sea. This is known as an undistributed middle term. So how about the next syllogism?

Celebrities like Posh and Becks have expensive weddings
We have a wedding we can't really afford
We are celebrities

Sorry deluded suburbanites. Posh and Becks spent millions on their wedding and are world famous. You've just wasted twenty grand and are no nearer celebrity status than you were before your wedding.

The royals go to Ascot
I go to Ascot
I am a royal

No, you pathetic snob, you're not a royal. It's that undistributed middle term again. The royals do go to Ascot but you and a whole lot of other oiks go there as well and you're certainly not royals.

Athletes wear trainers
I wear trainers
I am an athlete

No, like many people who wear trainers you're a fat, out-of-condition slob who would die if they had to run a race and wearing trainers doesn't make you any fitter.

Celebrities have famous birthday parties
I write 'JOE POTTS IS FIFTY' on some cardboard and leave it at the town roundabout
I'm a famous celebrity

No, you're not, dickhead.

Actually, most of the activities of modern society are based upon a pathetic faith in the undistributed middle. Advertising, for example.

Clint Eastwood wears jeans
I wear jeans
I am Clint Eastwood

Philosophy is not a comfortable intellectual ride. It's a subversive roller coaster that can leave you dizzy. Take cause and effect, for example. We all know what cause and effect means: A punches B on the nose which bleeds. A non-philosopher might conclude that A had caused B's nosebleed.

It ain't necessarily so, says your subversive, nit-picking philosopher. A's fist approaches B's nose. B reels backwards and blood flows from his nose. But where is the cause and effect? Isn't it possible that B slipped and had a nosebleed at the same time as A's fist swerved in his direction? Prove that it isn't.

Pretty silly reasoning you might think. Yet the world is a silly place. A parent takes her child to be vaccinated and after the injection the child has a fit in the surgery. "Your vaccine caused the fit," says the traumatised mother. "Oh no," says the doctor. "There must be something wrong with the kid." Doctors have been schooled in the nit-picking, philosophical distinction that just because there's *a temporal link* between the vaccine and an adverse reaction, just because they happen at the same time, this doesn't mean that the vaccine *caused* the adverse reaction. It was all the fault of the tiny patient—just like the man who had a nosebleed as an assailant's fist approached his nose.

In this way the weird, subversive, nit-picking mind-set of philosophers spills over into real life and medical practice and law suits.

What does philosophy teach us?

That we know bugger all.

A man called Descartes searched for ultimate truth, the most basic undeniable atom of truth. He would toss all the rotten apples of thought out of the philosophical barrel and leave only the freshest and best-preserved apple of all. After being locked away with a wood-burning stove all winter he came up with:

I think therefore I am or

Cogito ergo sum

Does 'I think therefore I am' seem reasonable enough to you, philosophical reader?

In fact, the *cogito* proves nothing at all. You think, do you? Well, this doesn't prove your physical existence for starters. You could be a ghost in some alternative universe thinking. Furthermore, if mystics are right and everything thinks, then thinking is no great deal and doesn't distinguish you from the nearest pebble.

Descartes might have more usefully inquired who his Latin teacher was.

These philosophers pull the roof off the house of reality and rip up the foundations with their logical diggers. They are never so silly, however, as when they start building a philosophical house of their own. Descartes was a disaster, a madman who cut the world in half. Mind and matter belong to different logical categories, he concluded and therefore—listen to this one—*thought cannot control the physical machine of the body.*

Ingenious philosophers thereafter wasted quantities of paper and decades of life on the ridiculous question: "How can the thought 'I will raise my arm' make my physical arm rise?" It was a major preoccupation of the 19th century, solemnly discussed at philosophical conferences, and in the 20th Century Wittgenstein, who wanted to drain philosophy an engineer drains a swamp, still worried away at this daft question in an unhelpful manner verging on behaviourism.

Descartes had an even more sinister effect upon science. If thought is divorced from matter then the physical world can consist only of mindless machines. There are many scientists today who, following the idiot Descartes, father of modern philosophy, believe we are machines! It's a dangerous belief! You can mothball a machine for years but you can't mothball a human without causing mental trauma. Machines don't suffer. People go mad!

Mind *does* affect matter. Of course it does! Of course thoughts control your body as hundreds of thousands of men jumping about parade grounds every day testify. The exercises in this book will affect your body.

If you want scientific proof of the relationship between mind and matter then take a look at quantum (a word which just means very small) experiments. There the mind of the scientist conducting the experiment becomes part of the experiment itself! Stuff you, Descartes!

So. Words are thought tarantulas. Nothing is provable. Maths is illogical.

What about data and statistics and graphs?

Well, there are lies, damned lies and statistics. One of the most glaring examples recently being the UN graph showing that fossil fuel consumption leads to global warming. This graph is shaped like a hockey stick, showing that global warming has dramatically accelerated together with fossil fuel consumption during the 20th century. All very well but the graph omits the medieval spike when global temperatures soared without a single car on the road. It also conveniently starts after a temperature spike 650,000 years ago when lions roamed Trafalgar Square. Furthermore 'climategate' revealed that the hockey stick curve is based on different data from the rest of the stick.

Are you enjoying this brief introduction to logic and Western philosophy, clever reader? You can't wait to get your hands on Bertrand Russell's introduction to western philosophy or Nietzsche's hilariously intelligent books such as 'Ecce Homo'? Who but Nietzsche would observe that German philosophy was the result of indigestion?

Or do you find it all a complete pain?

JO doesn't like this sort of thing. "Gonna go to Royal Ascot and be a royal, spend twenty K on the wedding and gonna wear trainers even if I'm as fat as a sofa. Yeah, yeah, yeah! Me and Clint. Me and Pink." That's JO.

But it won't do! Just look at Elvis, profoundly gifted, a Rock God who gave in to his JO's insatiable appetite for junk foods and prescription drugs and died ingloriously of constipation, his final moments spent frantically wrestling with a colon impacted with an immobile, clay-like sediment.

We live in a strange society where we can't take anything on trust. Politicians don't seem to work for the electorate anymore, we are sold junk foods which will attack the body's organs if eaten in sufficient quantity, drugs to cure obesity which can cause suicide, while our doctor might prescribe medications which have side effects which require other medications. If you're not careful you can go to the doctors with a back displacement and end up as a human chemistry set. A typical drug pusher doctor might put you on Prozac because you're depressed after having recovered from pleurisy as happened to a friend of mine.

I'm afraid poor JO just isn't fit to be set loose in modern society.

He may not like all this criticism and nit picking but it has to be done!

That very clever man the surrealist Salvador Dali had his critical-paranoiac method.

Sounds like a good idea to me. Be paranoid. Take nothing on trust, especially key words that govern our behaviour. "Go on, prove it!" Should be your credo when faced with popular beliefs.

Evolution? Prove it.

Global warming which has mysteriously segued to 'Climate Change'? Prove it.

Peak oil? Prove it.

Vaccines prevent disease? Prove it.

At a humble level know what you really are, know who you really are, know what your real interests are.

'Spiritual' books tell you to clear the deck of negative thoughts and enter a golden positive world where your positives will attract like positives and, without further effort, 'wishing will make it so' and you will become wildly successful. It's a little more complicated than that, I'm afraid. Incidentally, in the case of magnets a positive pole *rejects* another positive pole.

To get rid of all your negative thoughts means you have learned nothing in your life so far. I hope this isn't so! In assessing our beliefs we must distinguish between mere baggage and acquired wisdom. If you have been bitten by a dog as a child you might carry the 'all dogs are dangerous' baggage with you into adulthood. This is unhelpful as acting frightened with a badly brought up dog could earn you a nip and it also prevents you having a delightful, four-footed friend as a trustworthy companion.

'Staffordshire Bull Terriers are an intelligent dog and very good with children', has the mark of acquired wisdom, however. It's a *particularised* piece of information, mentioning a particular breed with particular characteristics. Similarly if a dude declares, 'Women are very dangerous creatures' the statement has the mark of baggage stemming from a traumatic sexual encounter whereas if another remarks, 'Brunettes bite harder than Blondes' you could discuss his acquired wisdom.

It's perfectly possible, clever reader, that like most of us you've picked up some delusional ideas over the years. Is it really the case that all members of the X party are greedy fascists while members of your own wonderful green humanistic Y party are the disinterested benefactors of mankind?

On the other hand 'The X party is only interested in the very rich but they hold excellent jumble sales,' has the mark of acquired wisdom.

You owe it to yourself to think clearly. Are those scientific beliefs of yours really scientific and evidence-based or just a form of propaganda you've innocently acquired, for example?

The mark of dodgy intellectual baggage is *VIOLENT EMOTION!* If an intellectual issue crops up in conversation and you find your Low Self longing to throttle the person who dares disagree with you then something is wrong. They say, 'never discuss politics or religion'—presumably because these issues are grasped in the white-knuckled hands of JO and rational discussion is therefore impossible.

'I think all this New Age health stuff about diet and healing is Old Hippy twaddle.' Time to look at the evidence.

'I think doctors just finish you off.' Time to look at the evidence.

If we regard ourselves as rational beings we should never be frightened of putting aside our prejudices and looking at the facts.

And acquired wisdom is wisdom, not prejudice. You should learn something in your life about people or your culture and come to sound conclusions or what's the point of living?

Remember:

'*Go for it!*' The voice of the Low Self.

'Look before you leap.' The voice of the Middle Self.

Exercise 12
Examining emotional baggage

Hot beliefs of ours in which JO plays too much of a part need examination if we're to claim to be rational beings.

(a) Identify a belief of yours that makes you hopping mad if it is questioned.
(b) Find out if it's true or not.
(c) Discuss a hot belief of yours with someone who doesn't believe a word of it reasonably without getting angry.
(d) Just because you believe something passionately doesn't mean that it's true or that it's untrue.

SIXTEEN
WHEN THINGS GO WRONG BETWEEN THE MIDDLE SELF AND LOW SELF

The relationship between the two souls is crucial to our health and happiness.

Here's what happens when that relationship goes wrong.

Sometimes we can just *ignore JO*.

Much of the unhappiness, much of the mental illness we suffer from, is caused by a breakdown in the relationship between the Low Self and the Middle Self, between the bio-computer of genius and the rational soul who sometimes thinks it runs the whole show.

One of our most basic mistakes—easily made when we've been told we're machines or that our JO is unconscious and inaccessible without ten expensive years on the couch—is to ignore the Low Self altogether. Unlike those JO People instinctively in touch with their Low Self many of us just ignore their inner child.

When the UK was a world empire it needed human machines to rule the world. The public school system would traumatise a child in a world of illicit sex and bullying and produced either a tough, mechanical beast who 'played the game' (Politician Douglas Hurd once described war-torn Bosnia as a 'level *playing* field.') or a broken, neurotic victim. Sensitivity was shut away in the sports locker. The empire builder, dissociated from his inner being, set the stiff upper lip tone for military and even middle-class families.

SNAP OUT OF IT
DON'T BE A BORE
DON'T WHINGE
PULL YOURSELF TOGETHER
PLAY THE GAME

Such advice amounts to war upon the Great Organiser.

A child subjected to the SNAP OUT OF IT treatment (Not uncommon in army families) can be caused horrific psychological damage. I have met female victims of such a military upbringing who have been so dissociated from their Low Self that they can never feel alive. Despite having husbands, family and money they are cut off from fully living and spend their time watching life on an old black and white TV with no sound, quite unable to connect with their inner being that gives emotional meaning to existence. By snapping out of it they have been reduced to a state of emotional dissociation.

It's not only military families who ignore their inner child, however.

CASE HISTORY

Mary, an attractive, young woman, came to see me after the end of one of my lectures. She was tearful. She said that my explanation of the Kahuna Low Self made her realise that she had been neglecting that inner self all her life. I asked her if she had any health problems and she said she had too many to mention, including arthritis. I gave her a few minutes healing.

When she came to see me for treatment she revealed that after leaving the meeting she had danced down the street, much to the amazement of her boyfriend who asked her what had happened to her arthritis. I suspected she had been suffering from hysterical arthritis caused by her Low Self which is capable of inflicting all sorts of medical problems. (Hysterical arthritis can include swollen joints.) Why had her inner child gone to such extreme measures?

It's rather a fascinating business examining someone's past mistakes in relation to their Low Self. It emerged that Mary had a dotty father with a volatile temper which had left her with the idea that she could handle difficult men. They were just like dad. As a consequence she married a violent man who would grab her by the hair and occasionally wield a knife. When he became menacing her Middle Self thought cheerfully, 'Oh, I can handle this. It's just like dad.'

Just as JO can record on the CCTV camera a more detailed version of reality than that perceived by the Middle Self, however, JO can also experience a dramatically different emotional reality and *drew her own conclusions from it.* Low Self conclusions can differ widely from the beliefs of the Middle Self. Thus while Mary's Middle Self was saying, 'It's all right. I can handle this.' Her JO was saying, 'Help! Get me out of here! This lunatic will kill us!'

The natural inclination of JO is to help and obey the Middle Self. When the Uhane starts leading JO into a load of grief, however, it causes trauma below. Mary's Low Self was being led in the battle of life by what appeared to be a lunatic. But the Great Organiser has one weapon in his or her arsenal: the Low Self controls the body's health. After years of suffering a desperate JO will try and drag the Middle Self to a halt and inflict, as a last ditch attempt, breathing problems, panic attacks, agonising pains, palpitations, hysterical arthritis—anything to ground the lunatic who is leading the body into disaster and possibly death.

Typically, the Low Self was continuing to inflict these health problems although Mary was now in a satisfying, non-violent relationship. After one session with me Mary, now taking positive charge of her JO, made an amazingly rapid turnaround which was immediately noted by colleagues at work.

SOMETIMES JO JUST DOESN'T KNOW WHEN TO STOP

JO's main purpose in life is to aid and help the Clever One. Lacking reasoning power, however, it is all too easy for the Great Organiser to install a programme into the bio-computer and then, although circumstances have completely changed, keep the redundant programme grinding away. The Low Self is trying to do his or her best but the results are a disaster. I was particularly close to such a case—which, as I hadn't discovered my own healing powers or read Max Freedom Long at the time, I didn't understand fully until some years later.

CASE HISTORY

My girlfriend Julie suffered from terrible, asthmatic, bronchial attacks when I first met her. It might be a sunny day, there might be a party on, but Julie could be confined to bed with a wheezing fit that nearly choked her. Her parents, literary and alternative people, had been believers in Nature Cure, that is letting the body be cured by natural methods, and as a result, Julie had seen very few doctors.

In those days I had a simple faith in medical science which I no longer possess—though Big Pharma can sometimes come up with the goods all right. "For God's sake!" I roared, faced with someone barely able to breathe. "Let's get you to a doctor and get this asthma or whatever it is sorted out!"

Julie was dragged sobbing to the doctor, prescribed an inhaler, took a couple of squirts and her bronchial asthma soon completely disappeared!

I now realise that bronchial inhalers don't cure asthma at all. (Healing, incidentally, cures asthma very easily or, if you want a more scientific approach, try the Buteygo Method). What on earth had happened? How had an inhaler, which at best merely manages the problem, cured such a severe case of bronchial trouble?

What had happened was this. Julie, daughter of impoverished literary parents, had been sent to the local village school. There the yokels had set about her, inviting the fluffy-haired artistic child to a 'bundle' on her first day at school. The bullying was so intense that Julie dreaded school like the plague. How could she escape this torture chamber?

Observing matters below her Low Self obligingly came to her aid. The only answer to the sadistic yokels who couldn't wait to torment little 'bird's nest' head was ill health and JO obligingly produced crippling asthmatic attacks. Breathing is closely related to our emotions and the bronchial tubes can rapidly reflect emotional problems. Take in and release a deep breath from the belly and you'll feel more relaxed, dear reader.

According to Professor Buteygo asthma is the result of nervous over-breathing which upsets the necessary balance of carbon dioxide and oxygen in the lungs, producing *too much oxygen*, and therefore fear and consequent hyperventilation can cause asthmatic symptoms.

Soon Julie was wheezing away at school time and mammy would have to keep her at home.

Job done! Her Low Self must have been pleased with her work. Unfortunately, being a JO, she had little reasoning ability. When school was long forgotten, when Julie was a backpacker, JO obligingly kept the asthma on tap and when Julie was settled with a companion, school a distant memory, JO was still at it. 'Don't worry, Julie, I've got plenty more bronchial asthma where that came from. You're safe.'

JO was watching when I roared that the doctor would fix things. Off to the doctors! Julie's Low Self had heard a lot about these strange medical personnel from her parents and here in the surgery was one at last, smelling of doctor, armed with his stethoscope, a battery of instruments gleaming all around him. JO found herself looking at the modern equivalent of a witch doctor. "I'll write you a prescription which should do the trick," says the witch doctor. "It's new on the market."

JO was suitably impressed. 'May as well give up on this asthma thing,' concludes the Low Self, admitting defeat. 'This is heap big magic.'

And the bronchial asthma disappeared over night.

JO JUMPS TO CONCLUSIONS

Sometimes JO can just misunderstand the nature of a problem entirely with disastrous results.

CASE HISTORY

Edward is a handsome young man, very spiritually aware, with everything to live for—yet plagued by an agonizing neurosis. He checks into a hotel, turns out the lights and is about to go to sleep when he hears distant, barely audible dripping. Instantly the curse of a panic attack returns. Adrenalin pumps, the heart thumps and sleep is out of the question. This emotional plague has followed him everywhere. The distant drone of an aircraft will spoil any retreat, the whirr of a neighbour's power tool make a house unliveable. Back at the hotel he rings and a staff member appears. The noise is virtually undetectable to either man. They concentrate. Edward beats it out and at last the hotel employee can hear it.

This neurosis which has followed him round the world and made his life a misery was based upon a simple misunderstanding by his Low Self.

Years ago Edward was sitting exams in which he was determined to triumph. A highly sensitive person he wanted to demonstrate that he was not woolly-minded but had a good brain. Unfortunately, he found himself sitting beside a radiator which transmitted hardly audible noises from a distant power drill. Small as the disturbance was it began to agonisingly interrupt the flow of his thoughts grappling with the exam. The more he tried to ignore the noise the more it distracted him and the greater became his mental distress. At last, finding himself totally agitated and unable to work he complained to a monitor about the noise and managed to have himself transferred to another room under supervision.

All is quiet. With relief he settles down to work again and is writing happily when he hears the distant drone of an aircraft. The more he tries to ignore it the more agitated he becomes and the more jumbled his thoughts. This vital moment in time when he hoped to succeed is being polluted by noise.

Observing the fear, the adrenalin, the agitation caused by the distant noise is his Low Self. 'Small noise bad and dangerous!' Concludes JO. 'But don't worry, beloved master. If I hear any of these small noises in the future you'll get good warning of them.'

It may seem a ridiculous mistake for JO to make but it isn't really. In our complex human world with its manifold technology anything at all can be the cause of panic—your computer producing the blue screen of death, for example. In a jungle war situation JO, by becoming hypersensitive, jerking you out of slumber and alerting you the faintest disturbance could warn you of the approach of an enemy and save your life.

Therefore Edward's JO in registering acute stress caused by barely audible noises was only trying to do his best.

I explained what was happening to Edward, counselled him repeatedly. It took a long time for the penny to drop but when Edward realised his neurosis was caused by a simple misunderstanding of his Low Self he reported to me in an awestruck tone of voice, "It's gone."

The neurotic curse had been lifted at last.

SEVENTEEN
A NERVOUS BREAKDOWN: JO TAKES OVER

A nervous breakdown is similar to shell shock in that it can involve JO pushing aside the Middle Self and commandeering the window of consciousness. In civilian life a nervous breakdown frequently occurs when life deals you a combination punch.

Let's say that Bill Average has a longstanding financial problem and has been finding it difficult to pay the mortgage for the last five years. Money is the lifeblood of society and the mortgage vampire has his hollow tooth into Bill's jugular but he grins and bears it and soldiers on. The stress causes impotence and the girl friend says she wants 'more space' and leaves. "How're you, Bill?" Friends ask. "I'm fine," he says, grinning and bearing it, having taken two jabs and frequent pummelling. And then one day while driving to work, he takes a corner too fast, over-corrects and land up in a hedge. This is the fatal uppercut accompanying the jabs.

"Oh no!" Says JO. "Too much! Oh no! Oh no! Oh no! I don't want to live this life no more!" And shoulders aside the Middle Self and grabs the window of consciousness.

In the days and weeks that follow Bill finds himself given to tears, panic attacks, likely to fall in love with any woman he meets, subjected to night sweats, irrational fears, weird thoughts, sleeplessness and burning pains.

A panic-stricken JO is now in charge of Bill who can't even look at mail without trembling and might do anything from sprinting up the hard shoulder of the motorway to hiding under the bed.

A nervous breakdown can continue for years. What is the answer?

The first step is to understand just what has happened and use the breakdown as an opportunity for self-development. You now are in intimate contact with your JO and you can learn all about him or her. This is what your Low Self is really like.

The night sweats, the irrational fears, the weird and wonderful symptoms have all been produced by poor old JO. They're not some form of primal curse or possession. The Great Organiser is just a mess when left in charge in real time.

The crew have mutinied and taken over the ship and got drunk. You're supposed to be the captain but you're floating in the bilge water below. My God! They'll have her aground!

What's to be done?

Somehow the captain's got to get up and wipe himself down. He's got to tell the crew that only he knows the way through these tricky shoals. Without him they'll end up in Davy Jones' Locker. He's got to reassert control.

Take Bill. He's got to realise that his weird symptoms (unless caused by the doctor's drugs) are produced by his Low Self, a Low Self which needs the help and guidance of the Clever One. After the accident his Low Self shies like a frightened horse at the sight of a car, for example. Time for the Clever One to point out that he's had fifteen years motoring without a single incident. Yes, he took a corner too fast but then no one else was injured and he has to drive if he is to work. We're going to buy a new car, Low Self, and learn to use it again. And you'll feel ever so much better when you can drive again.

The Low Self needs to be coaxed gently but firmly back under control and pushed away from the window of consciousness to become the Great Organiser in the background. The Low Self is a stubborn beast but can be controlled with perseverance and will.

I have counselled people back from a nervous breakdown and they find it a great relief that what they are experiencing is not a remorseless medical event but their own Low Self taking over and making a thorough mess of running the show. It's not a breakdown but a breakthrough if you play your cards right. Haven't you just been pushing yourself too hard, Bill? You thought you were tougher than you are. Make a more relaxed lifestyle for yourself. Remember: only you, the rational Middle Self can be captain of the ship. And take better care of Mr Silly Below who must never give the orders again!

EIGHTEEN
THE MOST IMPORTANT LOVE AFFAIR OF YOUR LIFE.
LOVING JO

Have fun
Ben Webster's last words

We don't want any of the disastrous mistakes chronicled in the previous chapter to happen to us, now do we?

Your most important love affair of your entire life is with yourself. Some of my patients, discovering that they house an emotional inner child who has been desperately devoted to them all their lives but who has been totally neglected, not to say, abused, became tearful.

It is now time to love your own inner being. If you can't this is bad news because loving oneself is a necessary step to loving others. They say that talking to yourself is the first sign of madness—whereas when we talk to ourselves we are only talking to our JO. Feel free to talk to yourself, either aloud or mentally, but now *you have to be very careful of what you say!*

Have you ever made a depressing remark aloud such as, "I don't think any man's going to look at me these days," and felt a pang of dismay down below? It came from her below, thoroughly depressed at the bad news. JO is always listening!

As we have seen a self-critical thought weakens the body's strength and repeated bad thoughts weaken the immune system. In World War I it was noted that regiments with low morale suffered more from trench foot, for example.

Your Inner Child, your younger brother or sister soul, your servant soul, your bio-computer, your little worshipful secretary looking after your nervous system and memory and health, a secretary who, even if totally illogical, can find out stuff the Clever One can't and is sometimes even in touch with the God Within has been neglected all these years! Pompous cultists like Richard Dawkins have persuaded you and almost everybody else that you haven't a soul. It's not your fault that your inner being has been ignored and neglected but now we've got to make up for lost time.

JO will be delighted to hear that he or she is going to be recognised and looked after at last and you will feel a response from within. It can be an emotional moment.

This relationship between Me and Myself is the most important relationship of your life. Remember: If you don't feel loveable then how can you accept love from another or love another? This is the relationship that brings happiness with it and makes life fun. What are the aspects of a loving relationship?

One important aspect of love is curiosity. In love we have an insatiable curiosity about the beloved. Music fans want to know the life story and day-to-day trivia of their idol and it is therefore perfectly natural for us to want to know more about our JO. As I suggested, writing your own Day in the Life can give us by introspection a great insight into JO's loves and phobias and strange habits of mind and also the extent to which the Low Self has already taken over our lives without the Middle Self realising it. Basic, honest introspection can tell us a lot about our inner selves. Finding our true animal self is another step forward and we can use the dowsing pendulum to question JO directly.

The first exercises in the book gave us vital clues to the character of the Low Self. As we have seen, JO is always listening and hates being criticised. He or she is so desperate to WINWINWIN that the thought of never winning the national lottery is painful. As will become clearer later when we describe the High Self and creativity, the Low Self has secret relations with the High Self, the God Within, and is therefore desperate to avoid any criticism of God! In the world of the Aumakua there is no division, no logic, no criticism and JO's phobia about criticism in general is a reflection of this.

Another aspect of love, as I have remarked in the context of loving children, is attention. If we love someone we attend to him or her and if we love our JO we attend to him or her. As we have seen the UK military and upper class (and those aspiring to be upper class) culture is based upon ignoring and brutalizing the Low Self, symbolised by sending the child off to an alien prep school environment at an age when the Low Self is at its most tragically vulnerable. 'Why on earth do these idiots continue to do it?' Rupert Everett asked in his superbly written autobiography when there's no empire left for traumatised zombies to rule.

When we love our Low Self (who is us after all) we attend to him or her and can be richly rewarded. JO can bring us early warning of health problems as he or she is in charge of the body's bio-computer. JO also has the ability to read the contents of other minds and is the psychic sounding board for occult information. Information about the bad vibrations in that house you're considering buying in is coming through JO and you'd better listen if you don't want to suffer in mental or physical problems in the property.

Another aspect of love is wholeness. We don't love on condition that or because of—we love the whole person, our entire country, all aspects of the activity of painting, say. One of the signs of being in love with a person is that we are thrown into a state of idiocy (from a Middle Self viewpoint) where we can't imagine they have any faults. So when we love JO we love all of JO in an unconditional fashion. An experience of love gives us a glimpse of the High Self where there is no division, where all is one.

Our love experience on the physical plane gives us only a glimpse of the Aumakua, however. If we love someone we want to possess him or her; in a state of love the last thing we want is our sexual partner to perform sex with someone else, for example. If we love our child then we can become equally possessive and therefore our love—unless it's truly disinterested love—can easily lead to conflict.

So how do we, the Clever One, the rational Middle Self, deal with the emotional volcano, the hysterical bio-computer below? The answer lies in the *parental* role of the rational Middle Self towards poor JO-who-can't-think-clearly down there. You should show your Low Self both a mother's indulgent love and a father's firm guidance (as these qualities were once understood). Imagine you are looking after a child.

"Mummy, will I die like grandma?"

"You'll go to heaven, darling,"

For there is one aspect of JO to bear in mind when dealing with him or her.

JO can't distinguish between fact and fiction.
JO doesn't know the difference between appearance and reality.

Don't believe me? Have you never been tense with suspense during a movie thriller or wept over a love story? I've got news for you. If there's a camera team taking close-ups, long shots and dolly shots then no one's in any danger. Clint Eastwood never shot anyone in his entire life. Janet Leigh wasn't stabbed to death in a shower. Kate Winslet was never on board the Titanic and sailed only a virtual ship. Yet, whatever the medium, be it the novel, the theatre, or TV our JOs happily confuse fact and fiction. Iago was likely to find himself dragged from the stage and attacked in theatrical productions in rural America. Valentino, despite dubious sexuality, was the heartthrob of millions of women. The actors who become TV soap stars are totally confused with the role they're playing by the public who will abuse the actor playing soap villains. Even the actors themselves can become confused between their role and who they really are (never a strong point with actors.). Someone masturbating to porn can go to sleep feeling they've had interesting sex. Stalkers can stalk stars convinced that they've been having a relationship with a celebrity they've never met, a relationship which has been mysteriously interrupted and just needs a little more persistence to be gloriously resumed.

Nor is this confusion a sign of stupidity. Flaubert famously vomited when writing the scene where Madame Bovary poisoned herself and Dickens 'became' the characters he was writing so that his son, overhearing Dickens writing the scene where Bill Sykes murders Nancy, thought a couple were violently quarrelling in his father's study.

And what's the vital importance of all this?

In talking to the Low Self you are dealing with an extremely powerful child. Take this whole question of winning and losing. We in western society have allowed ourselves to be made thoroughly miserable by having the carrot of mega-success dangled in front of our poor 'ordinary' noses until we feel painfully excluded from some wonderful superparty in the media skies where everyone just breathes success. Don't waste the best years of your life bewailing the fact that you're not a success—perhaps with perfect justification; goodness knows, several Shakespeares, Wagners and Blakes must have been trashed in today's shoddy world with its celebration of the mediocre or demented.

This is the secret: *Your basic happiness depends on the way you tell the story of your life to JO.*

I always remember meeting a little old lady, hobbling and shabbily dressed, who announced with such an innocent smile (I'm sure she wasn't putting me on), "I'm so lucky." She was totally convinced of her good fortune and hence her Low Self was serene and so she had a relationship with her Low Self much better than Elvis, for example, had with his.

"I have lived the American Dream," said Elvis at a press conference. "I have been Superman." He was a cool, manipulative character, dominating the Memphis Mafia who never knew which way he would jump and dating a string of glamorous women and, on a good day, appeared to be a buoyant, life-enhancing character, especially on stage where he embodied the genuine rock god, a smiling spiritual dynamo. His fans knew there was Love in the Air when the King rocked the house.

Yet the Low Self of Elvis clearly didn't feel lucky. His mum had died, he'd been creatively shafted by his own management and eventually Priscilla left him.

'Hush little baby don't you cry.
'You know your daddy was born to die.
'All my trials, Lord, will soon be over.'
And they were.

We don't want to make the tragic mistakes of poor Elvis, do we?—though in our case it would only happen to an 'ordinary' person.

The crucial role we adult Middle Selves play in loving him or her below is feeding JO the right thought-food. Some of us care about our diet yet fill our minds with thought junk food. We must filter and choose the information we want him or her down there to hear just as we would choose good nourishing food. We don't need to be dishonest—though it may be necessary to stretch the truth in certain circumstances—we just select the facts that are going to keep JO strong and happy and you will soon wake up the morning smiling. Before we get into positive thought let's start by giving JO the love he or she has been yearning for all these years.

Exercise 13
Loving JO

It's time to show JO just how much him or her is loved. Set a special JO evening aside and make it as cosy as possible with some photos of you looking young and happy and your favourite treats—musical, edible or watchable—available. You are not, however, to give JO that 'last' cigarette which is so desperately craved.

'I love you, JO and I just want you to know that I recognise you and I'm so grateful for all the work you've done for me over the years and I love you at last I'm now looking after all us now which is why I've stopped us smoking. We're going to eat only the best and tastiest foods and we're going to get really healthy. I'm going to start taking those vitamins and minerals to keep colds at bay. We'll never have another cold this winter with that Selenium tablet and Vitamin C. And I'm going to arrange as many treats for us as possible. I'm listening to you now and attending to your needs and I'll never neglect you again and we're going to have a wonderful time together. I'm going to buy that new dress (violent video for the male) and get us a Far Eastern cookery book (Karate course). The way you stopped me falling over when I tripped with the new juicer (warded off the blow when that guy tried to hit me) was phenomenal. I could have broken it (he could have killed me.) I'm sure you'd like some sex this evening and I have arranged just that. I love you, JO, I love you very much because you're Me, and you're part of the uniqueness that is my individual being. I'm sorry for not getting in touch sooner but now we're great friends and we're always going to be great friends and I have your real interests at heart.'

And remember:
NEVER—EVER—EVER PANIC JO WITH BAD THOUGHTS!!!

NINETEEN
CHILDHOOD TRAUMA, A BLOCK TO HAPPINESS

A more pernicious problem to deal with, a sort of built-in albatross, is childhood trauma. In childhood our JO is out there on the street, totally unprotected, drawing universal conclusions from a particular experience. If a child's mother is a drunken slob the young child has no standards for comparison and naturally concludes that motherhood consists of drunken slobbery. When that child grows into adulthood (whatever that is) we now encounter another problem.

The Low Self, which as we have seen is a powerful beast generating our emotions, often uses reality merely to *confirm* what it already 'knows'. For example, a JO convinced all mother are drunken slobs, will dismiss motherly mothers as 'sentimentalists acting the role of mother' or remain convinced that proper mothers become drunken slobs when everyone's back is turned. This traumatised JO will then consort with drunken slob women to experience 'reality'.

The adult Marlon Brando while womanising wasn't just looking for sexual pleasure; he forced women to conform to his mother's derelict version of femininity by constantly awakening their deeper emotions and then betraying them when they loved him. Hell hath no fury like a woman scorned and naturally the dames struck back. He cheated on one of his favourite women whom he could have had a great relationship with had it not been for his childhood trauma and she got her own back on Brando by *seducing his son*. Gotcha!

We are all of us dragging a load of emotional baggage in our life and some of it may be of a traumatic nature.

As soon as you become aware of your Low Self you're either a very lucky person or you will realise that poor him or her below has been mauled over the years. As we have seen, childhood has probably imprinted JO with all sorts of foolish prejudices and conditioned our behaviour for life. A doting mother can condition a young man with the belief that all women want to look after baby—a delusion which can have disastrous consequences. The Low Self can be a very stubborn character and the lessons of childhood are not easily unlearned.

Poor Brando calls his amusing autobiography 'Songs my mother taught me', pathetically clinging to some positive legacy from the neglectful drunk who was his mother. The vicious and neglectful parent can infuse their child's entire world with a bitter poison which a lifetimes' success sometimes fails to cleanse. As Brando put it he couldn't think, act, drink or screw himself out of an abiding sense of unworthiness and depression. Success, so sought after by the entire western population, was to him an empty delusion. He was also drawn to movie roles where he was beaten, flogged or killed as if to relive childhood pain.

Is it possible to unlearn childhood conditioning? Supposing as a little girl your father didn't love you and you've been left feeling unlovable. This makes you chose unsuitable men to repeat the non-love situation to confirm what the Low Self already 'knows'. You learn later in life that your father couldn't love you because he was totally unloved by *his* mother, and hence couldn't relate to women and this is how you're wired to react in this destructive, repetitive fashion.

There's not going to be a quick and easy fix for such a difficult emotional problem unless through the High Self. Otherwise the rational Middle Self is faced with a long retraining battle. First you need an overview of the situation—it was the fault of your father's blasted mother and the curse is still working. Even now you're getting the hots for this exciting-looking man but you know rationally that he's cold and manipulative and married and it will be a disaster just like a previous affair which dragged on for far too long and you're not getting any younger.

It can be a lengthy educative, retraining process to fix an ingrained problem of this sort. Freud seemed to think that merely digging up the trauma from the 'unconscious' and confronting the patient with a personal disaster he had forgotten was therapeutic, whereas awareness of the problem is the first important step but is unlikely to constitute a cure in itself—unlike those psychoanalytical movies where to merely understand the cause of your destructive behaviour is to be cured overnight. In fact, the Middle Self has to constantly counsel the Low Self. 'I'm sorry for all the pain you the Low Self have endured and your abiding sense of lovelessness but there is a way out, a way forward . . . We can't go on making the same mistake, endlessly choosing the wrong person and then suffering for it . . .

The time has arrived to form a stable and healthy relationship with a member of the opposite sex . . .'

A lengthy process of observation and retraining of JO is needed here and it's not going to be easy unless . . .

One answer to the parental curse came in Dr Steven Greer's mind-boggling memoir 'Hidden Truth—Forbidden Knowledge.' As well as being author of the Disclosure Project and a brilliant ER surgeon, Dr Greer is a man of remarkable spiritual powers. He emerged unscathed from a horribly abusive childhood wherein he was once driven to eat soil for nourishment! When he and his sister saw 'Mommy Dearest' about the horrors of being Joan Crawford's daughter they commented that a day with Crawford would have been a good day for them!

Yet Dr Greer shrugged all the childhood horror aside and became a totally positive individual.

How did he do it?

As a youth he fell sick with septicaemia, had an out of the body experience and sailed straight into the World Mind, the glorious congregation of the world's Aumakuas. Blazing Love from Above dissolved and banished the emotional paranoia associated with that terrible childhood and healed his spirit. He became a great ER doctor and happy family man.

Can we all lose our traumas like that? Steven Greer is a man of exceptional psychic gifts and it's doubtful we can all have such an immediate resolution of terrible problems. He tells an amusing anecdote about going on a meditation course which was supposed to enable the student to reach *samahdi*, a state of union with the High Self. Steven began his mediation and the teacher observing him exclaimed with astonishment, "You're actually doing it!" Which says a lot both about Steven Greer's psychic ability and the outcome of many a psychic course which is largely dependent upon the student's own gifts.

Undoubtedly the quickest way out of our traumas and emotional difficulties *is* through the High Self which we all possess. It's well worth it to try and make contact with the God Within, however fleeting and ephemeral it may seem at first, and once we can contact the Aumakua it's remarkable how manageable emotional difficulties become. Do you have a friend who is a High Self person? High Self types, however other-worldly their views, don't suffer from childhood trauma in the self-destructive, obsessive fashion that those lower down the psychic scale do. There's a lesson here. That Christian stuff about forgiving your enemies begins to make sense at last—from a mental health point of view, anyway. Rather than wishing dad was still alive so you could give him a good kicking what about rewriting history and forgiving him? . . . Perhaps he wasn't such a bad sort now you understand everything . . . Perhaps mum really loved you after all . . . That time you fell off your bike and hurt your knee didn't she pick you up? . . . Remember that the Low Self can be persuaded of anything at all. Time to don your High Self hat and start rewriting history . . .

Exercise 14
I'm so lucky

Remember Herman Melville's point that we always seek to claim superiority over others. It's not such a bad idea to humour JO in this hard-wired desire for superiority which has undoubtedly existed since the species began. It's time to don rose-coloured spectacles and rewrite the rich and wonderful saga of your life. Remember how JO has difficulty distinguishing reality from fantasy anyway.

"How lucky I am to find you at last JO thanks to this wonderful book by Joe Potts which I was given for my birthday. Of course, we've always been lucky. Think how lucky we are to be born at all, those millions and millions of sperm fighting to get to the little egg and one lucky sperm making us out of all the other possibilities. There must be a good reason for our unique personality to make it through the sperm race! And what good fortune to be born in this present age with modern medicine which saved our life when we caught pneumonia at the age of 12. Could have been gone then but we're still here at 33, a peak age where we're still young but have the seeds of wisdom. What a stroke of luck also to be born in an age where the great singers and musicians of the world are there for us at the press of a button! No, we're not a showbiz success but that's irrelevant to normal people leading real lives and look what a mess some of these showbiz types like poor River Phoenix make of their lives! Heath Ledger dead of prescription drugs and what an idiot Britney Spears has made of herself. I've got a great relationship with my parents and two great kids. And one day I may surprise them all with my achievements . . ."

Incidentally, education, unless it's a practical qualification, can equip you with nothing but false hopes. Most Oxford graduates are disappointed with their post university careers. You've got an Oxford First and you never became Jeremy Paxman and the stress has left you with M.E. Isn't it wonderful though that a grateful UK is paying you money just to laze about the place, however? Think of the sex you can have! And there's so much for you to learn! So begin your real education now. That Oxford stuff was just a dream. Once you start to enjoy yourself your ME (if it's the stress-induced sort) will disappear. Every health problem has a cure if you're prepared to look for it long enough. You're really a very lucky human animal. Any other society would have just knocked you on the head! And what can you sensibly do with your paper qualification? Use it perhaps to start a completely new career.

Once you become aware and observe modern Western society with all its welfare and medical safety nets and libraries and bizarre technology it seems like an extraordinary playground. What a lucky little human animal you are! Let's start leading a life of quiet happiness instead of the noisy despair of the disappointed booby tricked by admen!

You will have achieved your end when you can say with the poor old Lady and without a trace of irony, 'I'm so lucky.'

TWENTY
POSITIVE THOUGHT POSITIVE THOUGHT POSITIVE THOUGHT

Positive thought is manna to the Low Self and should be applied, not only to our personal history, but all aspects of life. Yet positive thought is lost in a minefield of cliché, misrepresentation and humour. What could be more hilariously positive than Monty Python's song of the crucified, 'Always look on the bright side of life'?

Is the glass half full or half empty?

To which Woody Allen replies, 'For me the glass is always empty, not half full, just empty.' Unfortunately, it's not a joke and the privileged old grump means it. Positive reader, if you're going to get anywhere psychically that darn glass has got to be brimming half-full!

Positive thought can also be lost in a ridiculous American-style optimism, a can-doism which assumes that the big bad physical world can always be made to conform to the *will* of the can-doer. One lady can-doer, stated brightly, "After all, cancer is only cancer!" Yes, and chemotherapy is only chemotherapy and death is only death.

Satirised or unconsciously parodied by American can-do-ism, positive thought is yet crucial thought-food for the Low Self. This vitally important, yea-saying can range from simple methods of positive thought practised by 'ordinary' folk ('Tomorrow is another day') to the sophisticated exercises advocated by John Cowper Powys in 'The Art of Happiness'—a book, incidentally, which rescued me in my youth as I was about to sink into a swamp of hysterical self-pity.

But do you actually want to be happy, dear reader?

It's time to be honest with ourselves.

Do you really, really, really want to be happy?

Or are you 'half in love with easeful death?' If you even half *want* your misery, if you indulge it at all, if you think your misery is the real truth of the damned situation, is more sophisticated, is more cool, if you've got even so much as a toe in the inviting quicksand of self-pity, then this positive thinking just isn't going to work.

'It's so unfair . . . if only . . . poor, poor me . . . it wasn't my fault . . . it's so damned unfair . . . I don't deserve this . . . I did my best . . . I'm a good person . . . why are others so much luckier than me when they're rotten people and I'm a good person? . . . if only . . .'

It *is* unfair . . . it *didn't* turn out right . . . you *are* a poor you . . . it *wasn't* your fault . . .

And no one gives a damn . . . except you! Our JOs can be quite ruthless. We avoid failure as it were catching. Other humans will just find your misery a complete bore—unless they love you or they're actually *enjoying* your misery. Could it be you're feeding their competitive streak and your misery is just making the devils feel superior? As Dostoyevsky points out in 'The Gambler' "People really like seeing their best friends humiliated; a great part of friendship is based upon humiliation; and this is an old truth known to all intelligent people."

Whatever the injustice of the situation, whatever life could have been, it isn't and here we are, what is is, and we have the choice either to sink to the bottom of the swamp or swim forward with the Kahunas!

Feeling sorry for yourself? Tempted to let go splat into that inviting quicksand of self-pity strewn with dead hopes, bubbles of amplified misery and anti-depressants? *Don't do it!* Ultimately, you're just going to have to drag yourself out the gooey mess anyway.

In the quicksand already? Well, poor you, whatever the injustice of your fate, you will have to exert positive choice and grab a floating branch and crawl back through that sorry, slimy stuff with its broken dreams and betrayals and bad luck and drag yourself out of the inviting slobber of self-pity onto dry land of reality.

Self-pity can lead a person badly astray like the man who jumped off the Golden Gate Bridge and realised as he was falling that all the difficulties in his life could be fixed apart from the fact that he had jumped off the Golden Gate Bridge. (In his case luck hadn't deserted him and he survived.)

Time passes. Remarkably quickly. We're not here for ever. Do you want your life to be dragged down by the stupid self-indulgent quicksand of self-pity? Or do you want to be alert, empowered, fully focussed on what is a unique moment of your conscious life in eternity?

Of course, you do. You want to exert positive will. You want to be happy.

Remember, happiness is the happiness of JO! The reason the Poor Old lady felt so lucky was that she had a good relationship with her Low Self. The reason Elvis had to feed his inner beast with junk food and dose it with prescription drugs was that he'd fed it sad ideas and had a bad relationship, an indulgent relationship, with his JO. He'd lost sight of the big picture. He needed intelligent Middle Self advice about the dangers of prescription drugs.

The Middle Self has the power of CHOICE.

SO CHOOSE.

The world is what you think it is. How sad and how common it is to look back upon your life and say, "That was a pretty good life when I was young but I was so hung up about X that I was depressed all the time. And X didn't really matter in the end."

What albatrosses we hang around our necks!

So goodbye albatross!

Is this positive thought only self-delusion? Is there a *real* world advancing on us all like a remorseless social steamroller?

Consider the case of artists Blake or Turner, the former an eccentric failure, the latter a prosperous celebrity artist, living in the 'real' society of the eighteenth and nineteenth centuries which was completely out of step with their technical and spiritual artistic innovations. They were both thought to be mad. Now, however, whereas the once acceptably bland artists of the eighteenth and nineteenth centuries are forgotten, Blake and Turner are cultural giants. It seems the values of the real eighteenth century world weren't so real after all.

If future biographers look back on the present age they are likely to select artists that we treat as nobodies as important subjects.

Despite his exhilarating energy Elvis was 'half in love with easeful death'. In that performance of 'Suspicious Minds' in 'Elvis on Tour', for example, Elvis is a magnificent, joyous rock god bursting with energy yet he riffs, in a hypnotic, half-improvised passage, 'caught in a, caught in a trap, caught in a trap'. He needed to dwell more on his gifted good fortune and not to cling to the setbacks in his life, some of which were self-inflicted. From the purely selfish fan point of view, of course, this self-defeating, tragic element adds to the depth of the King's musical appeal.

Compare Elvis with Chuck Berry. "I'm not figuring on dying," snapped Berry to Keith Richards when the latter explained he was trying to improve Berry's music so there'd be good music left when Berry was gone.

Have you told yourself 'I have failed'? Either you're old and tired and failed or young and furiously angry and failed. FAILURE is a label guaranteed to send JO into decline.

It's most important to avoid the F-word and create a hopeful worldview. Don't tell JO. 'I've had it! I'm cooked!' Suppose you're a not-so-young actor working at Walmart instead of making it in Hollywood as the new De Niro. Don't kill yourself with booze and drugs. The world of acting is a crazy lottery. The reason Humphrey Bogart looked so raddled, apart from doing a massive amount of sex, was that he (and Bette Davis) failed to make it in Hollywood in his younger days. Perhaps you'll make your mark in middle or even old age. Don't smother your own dreams.

'Live in hope though you die in despair.' Many of these old saws contain a great deal of positive wisdom. Hope is food for JO.

Early success is a danger. Look at poor River Phoenix. At least you're better off that him. You've got a long way to go and you love growing plants. Do the things that you can succeed at and become a great gardener. Spread your net of achievement wider. Live now.

You are your attitude.

You are what you think.

Society is not a great steamroller advancing on you but a shifting mirage, a mirage that you can shape to your own purpose. When you look back on the past it is quite apparent that it *was* a mirage, a mirage that you could have made much better use of.

'Row, row, row your boat gently up the stream . . .

'Merrily, merrily, merrily, merrily . . .

'Life is but a dream . . .'

It takes energy to be depressed which is why depressed people become happy when illness reduces their energy. Depression is negative thought producing negative energy rather like Reich's Deadly Orgone (DOR) whereas positive thought produces positive energy like Orgone, the life force. You don't want to use your energy and all the resources of society to produce only a black cloud of DOR, do you?

TWENTY-ONE
THE UNIQUE INDIVIDUAL

'As kingfishers catch fire, dragonflies draw flame;
'And tumbled over rim in roundy wells
'Stones ring; like each tucked string tells, each hung bell's
'Bow swung finds tongue to fling out broad its name;
'Each mortal thing does one thing and the same:
'Selves—goes itself; **myself** *it speaks and spells,*
'Crying **What I do is me: for that I came.***'*

Gerard Manley Hopkins 'Inversnaid'

I have a friend who considers that record companies stole several famous songs from him.

"They took away my identity, Joe," he said.

I couldn't understand what he meant at first.

If one's work is stolen then you would lose royalties and status in life but your identity is you, the unique interaction of the three souls that is your psychic being.

I've always had a sense of who I am, an intuitive closeness to my Low Self and later an intellectual cultivation at least of the Middle Self. However ridiculous others might find my point of view, I have always regarded my feelings and conclusions as the benchmark by which I judge society rather than regarding my place in the pecking order of society as a judgement upon my personal value. What my friend was talking about was his *social* identity.

It seems to me a dangerous mistake to confuse the two. It can be as dangerous for the successful as the unsuccessful. Whereas we 'ordinary people' gawp with obedient envy at celebrities being one can be a tough call. In a recent TV programme ('Surviving Gazza' Jan 2009) the footballer's fame seemed to have resulted in psychosis as well as alcoholism for he was seen in a pub boasting that the Pope and famous politicians were in constant touch with him and on a visit to his family he revealed a worrying obsession with numerology. Paul Gascoigne the father and human being and owner of a vulnerable liver had been completely usurped by the tabloid Gazza identity just as a schizophrenic can be possessed by the identity of Napoleon.

The privacy of our own identity is something we have to guard in certain circumstances. Ideally we share it with others such as family members and friends but if you want to make it in the social world it's wise to pretend to be a conformist (unless non-conformism is fashionable). For all its soft-soaping of 'wonderful you the individual consumer and democratic voter' society requires conformists and worker ants to get the job done. So keep your individuality under wraps until such a time as you can afford to let him or her out on the street.

We must never fall into the trap of thinking the Low Self is some foreign power occupying our minds like the non-existent Freudian 'unconscious'. No. The Low Self is part of your unique individuality and every Low Self is different.

Some JO's are just better at sports than others, for example.

When John McEnroe was a child his JO was just so good at tennis people thought at first sight that Little John was a tennis-playing dwarf. And if your Low Self isn't up to the job, forget it. Like poor old Henman whose Low Self was never up there in the tennis wizard class. Unless all his opponents died in a mid-air collision he'd never have won Wimbledon. It's not a question of will or character; it's a question of your Low Self psycho-physiological equipment.

And in sports as elsewhere JO can take off and lead a life all of his or her own. Sometimes, McEnroe reports, that little tennis ball seemed as big as a watermelon and he just couldn't possibly miss such a huge fat target. Not that John McEnroe's Middle Self could make the tennis ball into a 'melon' at will. Unless you're a yogi in complete control of mind and body and can inhale your stomach to your backbone, JO has his or hers ups and downs.

The same applies to music. Django Reinhardt had a JO who was astonishingly good at playing the guitar, even after losing the use of two fingers of his chording hand in a fire. It's not that other guitarists don't want to play guitar as well as Django and don't practise just as hard to achieve that. Their Low Selves just aren't up to either the gypsy's technique or phenomenal powers of melodic and harmonic improvisation.

Which is not to say that the naturally-talented sportsman or musician doesn't need the reasoned guidance of the Middle Self—in finding a suitable coach, for example, or making tactical decisions as to how to outwit a particular opponent. *This is why the collaboration of the two selves is so important—in life as well as in sport.*

Tina Turner is gifted with an awesome vocal power and could start a concert on a climax and end it over an hour later on a crescendo. She could make Mick Jagger sound like a mouse when he sang with her. Incidentally, Tina Turner channelled the vital force which we'll mention in a later chapter and was fascinated by its power.

In war individuals also differ dramatically. The natural warrior retains his morale during the boring and depressing interludes of war and lovingly polishes his weaponry while others conclude this is a hellish business and they're probably going to die. When the bullets whistle past many soldiers sensibly 'eat dirt' but there are those lions of men who somehow make it to the enemy pillbox and drop a 'pineapple' inside.

Sport, music and war are just some of the dramatic ways in which individual Low Selves differ. We also differ in our degrees of aggression, competitive urge or capacity for love. Let's face it: some Low Selves are much nicer than others. Sadism and masochism are perversions only in extreme forms. The masochist who destroys everything of value in his life and then commits suicide or the serial killer are perversions of a perversion whereas all of us exist somewhere along the sadism-masochism spectrum. To enjoy self-knowledge we must know where we ourselves figure. You could give yourself a masochism and sadism number from 1-10 and then dowse your place. (See Dowsing)

Leaning from a window of the Chelsea hotel Quentin Crisp mused that everybody in New York was frantically chasing one thing, success, and yet all they had to do to be an instant success was realise their own individuality—as he did himself by dressing as pioneer freak when cross-dressing wasn't done at all. Become what you are instead of what others say you should be and you are already a success.

Exercise 15
Reclaiming your own

(a) Look at your face in the mirror and say, 'This is my face, my individual face and I take back my face from society.' Enhance your own appearance instead of conforming to the fashion of the day.

(b) Look at your body in a mirror and say, 'I take back my body from society. This is my voluptuous, individual body and I'm damned if I'm going to try to look like a stick insect.' If you want role models you've got the history of cinema to find a heroine that suits you as your icon.

(c) Say, 'I take back my soul from society.' There are many tips in this book as to discovering who you really are, how rational you are or who wins in your life—your rational self or your animal self. Then there's the question of whether your High Self has made an appearance. The complex interaction of the Trinity of Mind is your identity. It is important you finds a role, great or small, in society (Though how many of us like Louis Armstrong, a successful musical genius, can declare, "My life has been all joy."?) but if you don't find a suitable social role and you feel like round peg in a square hole then don't despair or lose respect for the individual you are. Cherish your individuality which can be lost in success as well as failure.

TWENTY-TWO
GETTING THE BEST OUT OF SOCIETY

We can't ignore society. We are hard-wired to WINWINWIN and society is our battleground. We are also dependents on a whole history of technological ingenuity which society lavishly bestows upon us.

This book does not suggest you abandon ambition—far from it. Go for it, ambitious reader, and your chances of success will be greatly enhanced with your three souls acting harmoniously. Unfortunately, however, 'most men lead lives of quiet despair' as Thoreau put it, because, of course, their youthful dreams have been shattered.

The advice to 'Live your Dream' can be a recipe for both economic and emotional disaster.

In the case of most of us the bigger your ambitions the bigger the mountain of crap you're building for yourself.

The problem is that society from schooldays onwards presents us with an increasing number of higher and higher hurdles to jump. In a tribal or village society it was possible for everyone to have a role and be successful in that role in that micro-society. You could be successful as a mother breeding the biggest and strongest labourers in the village, as a baker baking the best loaf of bread or even as the village idiot sweeping the yard. No one suggested you should apply for the job of king or even squire who seemed like different species of human being. Amusingly, someone owning an estate in Dorset today still manages to appear like a different species to the cap-doffing locals.

In the complex society of today, however, the hopes and egos of everyman are pumped up like barrage balloons. 'Come on,' says the media circus barker. 'Win the Lottery, become a Celebrity, a Rock Star or even Prime Minister and now even black men can become president.' Alas, the chances of success in any of these fields are millions to one against us whatever our ability.

In the political field our chances as a voter of making our needs felt are also ridiculously overblown. The politician informs us we are an 'all-powerful member of the democratic world community' when, in fact, unless we become an activist, our political power amounts to little more than an opportunity to scream at the TV.

As we crash and burn in society's obstacle course we can make a dreadful mistake. We turn on ourselves in disgust—which means the embittered Middle Self turns on poor little Great Organiser who has been doing his or her best in trying to help us to be a new Paul McCartney, Amy Winehouse, Johnny Depp, Kylie Minogue, Robbie Williams, JK Rowlands, Richard Branson or win the lottery. 'What's going on up there?' Asks Poor JO in horror. 'I've done my very best and now the Clever One is tearing his hair out! Ouch! He says I'm a useless idiot! Oh no! He wants to jump off a bridge! What have I done wrong?'

All this self-abuse must end. *We must unite with our Low Self—Uhane and unihipili must be staunch friends and allies facing whatever society and people can throw at us.* Together we stand, Me and Myself, divided we fall, in giving life our best shot. After all, if we fail at the ridiculous high jump which society has lured us into attempting, then we're simply part of the vast majority of humans who've been teased by media manipulators. Real life can now start.

There are, of course, ambitions which are well within our scope, real objectives which can be obtained by hard work or cunning. An aware and united Middle Self and Low Self stand a much better chance of realising these than if these two souls are at odds.

Whatever our social success our failure, however, we can still be happy—Our Low Self is waiting for our lead here.

The Low Self is a conscious soul, easily persuaded of anything, waiting for our direction! Lead your Low Self towards happiness. If the Middle Self tells JO that all is well then our Low Self will be content (unless the bailiff arrives or the bomb goes off, of course).

Start living life to the full—after all, none of us are getting any younger. Life is a most extraordinary gift and we should be both aware and appreciative of nature's bounty.

It's most important to unite with your Low Self in the battle of life and crucial to feed your Low Self with the very best mental food.

Get the best out of society. Beware of group thinking. Is it such a good idea to wreck your education with your yobbish behaviour like your schoolmates when you need all the skills you can get in today's world? Beware of trends. What was 'Girlie Power', but the 'power' of giving sex away (instead of cannily rationing it) and puking in the gutter alongside a man who doesn't know how to hold his booze either? Do you really need that new car or could it wreck your finances? And when 'Your Country Needs You' it's time to run.

Society still has its mind-forged manacles ready even if they're called consumerism or attitude or benign government. Cast them aside. Be you.

Play our mental cards right and there's no reason at all why we shouldn't declare, 'Most people lead lives of quiet joy.'

TWENTY-THREE
POSITIVE WILL

"When the mind says, 'Walk' the body walks."
Frederick the Great

Before any of this is going to work you have to *will* it to work. Sometimes nice people fail because they just can't generate enough will power. If you haven't got positive will it's time to generate some.

I know some incredibly fit 80-year-old activists who drag their shopping up and down hill instead of using the car. This is a different attitude to JO, the attitude of the firm father rather than the indulgent mother where you saddle up the Low Self and say, 'You can do it.' A healing patient of mine related how he got himself walking again on damaged feet which doctors despaired of—impelled only by a fear of losing his job.

Making yourself perform a daunting physical task will increase your domination of the Low Self and you will realise you're not as feeble as you thought. Mental tasks have the same effect. You *can* read 'War and Peace'. You *can* influence others. You have to say something to your mother about her making a will. Sometimes you can just stifle yourself with your own inhibitions and be afraid to speak up for yourself in private or in public. Once you discover you *can* address a meeting you might fall in love with the sound of your own voice. Overcoming social inhibitions is a step forward in making your presence felt.

Weakness and delay can make a problem grow like a giant puffball. When we delay filling in that income tax form the darn thing just seems to get more and more incomprehensible and threatening. Go to the Citizens' Advice or ask even the taxman for help. Get it done. Tackle unpleasant tasks.

Remember, the Middle Self is the Captain and JO the willing crewmember.

TWENTY-FOUR
HUMOUR

Sometimes it seems that God just invented the human race to have a good laugh.

There is something of the Divine in humour.

Even such a formidable psychic such as Dr Steven Greer felt humour helped him beat cancer.

Never lose your sense of humour. The banana skin awaits the noblest of us. The poet Yeats, who regarded magic as important as poetry, attended many a séance but at one particular event, when the spirit spoke through an attractive female medium, it was not what the Nobel Prize winner wanted to hear. Speaking through the medium the spirit declared that Yeats was a lecher who wanted to seduce the poor young lady. Imperturbably, the Poet and adept of the Golden Dawn declared that a foul spirit had come through.

If someone could just move the table he would make the necessary signs of banishment on the carpet.

The table was moved and Yeats made some impressive Golden Dawn inscriptions on the floor with his silver-headed walking stick.

"Don't think you frighten me with that jiggery-pokery," said the spirit. "I know just what you want to do with that mutton dagger of yours."

It's a good idea to realise that, however serious our intentions, we are all ridiculous to a greater or lesser degree and we should take a humorous view of our difficulties. Laughter is a strange and wonderful human characteristic which can both discharge hoarded stress and give a ribald positive glow to otherwise terrible circumstances.

There are many stories of people, apart from Dr Greer, who have been cured of dire diseases by getting their favourite comedy videos out and laughing all weekend.

TWENTY-FIVE
CREATIVITY

Creativity is the greatest drug of all and it doesn't have to involve the traditional fields such as writing, music and painting. Creativity is basically problem solving. Gardening, starting a little business, even selling at a car boot has an element of problem solving and creativity. Somehow our JO goes to sleep happily if there's some creative problem to be solved tomorrow.

Something astonishing can happen during sleep. The writer Robert Louis Stevenson while asleep used to have help from what he called his Brownies for story ideas and would wake up with a ready-made plot. And what brilliant archetypal ideas his Brownies provided. 'Dr Jekyll & Mr Hyde', for example, which is a fable of how the Low Self, neglected and suppressed by the pious Middle Self of a scientist, turns into a violent monster. The characterisation of JO in the fable is spot on; Mr Hyde isn't evil, just impatient like any healthy Low Self and violent when frustrated.

Stevenson's Brownies were neither from the Middle Self or the Low Self; any writer struggling to invent a good idea knows only too well how frustrating this can be and most dreams are just surreal boring tosh. This leaves only one possibility. Stevenson was getting help from the Aumakua in the night as the God Within passed on wonderful ideas to the Low Self. This is why painters and writers often struggle on with their craft despite poor money because, without knowing it, their satisfaction comes from contact with the God Within. It also explains why JO is so frightened of offending God with Whom he has intimate contact.

Just as creativity can be a reward in itself and keep an artist happily occupied in old age, creative frustration can be a killer. The sheer *cool wit,* as well as the exhilarating projection of vital force of Elvis's performance, have never been bettered. Yet this brilliant and passionate vocal pioneer ended up trashing the songs that Bob Dylan sent him and singing 'Old McDonald had a Farm'. He'd lost his creative vision completely.

After cleaning up the prescription drug habit and junk food and realising that even Superman has to cope with the blues, a wise Elvis would have decided, 'I'm going to make some great records and great movies and see the world, man.' And Elvis, who was a formidable *spiritual* force, would still be with us today.

Creativity is a religion without a religion.

Give yourself a creative project and wake up happy in the morning.

PART TWO

ONE
THE STORY SO FAR

We learn through pain but we live through pleasure

Our little spiritual boat is launched willy-nilly on the torrent of life and has probably been battered by the Gales of Experience. Whether we have been sailing in society's Ship of Fools, whether we still wish to take to the high seas, or whether we fancy sailing on Lake Placid, I assume you are now fully in charge of your own vessel. You have discovered that wondrous yet foolish inner being, your very own Low Self whose astonishing abilities as a bio-computer are only equalled by a judgemental idiocy which makes him or her perfect fodder for the adman or the politician leading us to ruin. But you now have the measure of JO and what a difference it makes to be in control of this formidable character.

Once your JO would be stampeded by the TV news or lured into smoking or a time-consuming and expensive competition with the airbrushed image of a physical freak in a magazine. Now your face and your body are your own and not a plaything of society. Now you realise you are as young and beautiful as you're likely to get and had better enjoy it while it lasts. Once you felt inferior because you never went to university but now you realise it's not important at all and the business you built up gives you a better life-style than most graduates whose education has done little more than inflate their egos to bursting point.

You are now in touch with the realities of life. And what a strange reality it is! You are a human animal with three souls, one of them much more powerful than you could ever have dreamed of. You live in a society that can be amazingly generous as a provider of education, welfare and technology and yet is out to destroy you spiritually and lead you by the consumer nose through diminishing circles of materialism.

You are aware of and respectfully recognise the animal nature of your Low Self. Animals are not the machines of scientific fiction but can experience stress, love, even vanity and they possess more telepathic abilities than most humans. Animals have a lesson for us all. A dog is always ready to enjoy life to the full when given the opportunity. Contrast the dog's relish of life with ours. While the dog is eagerly reading smells as we might read a beautiful poem we are likely to be worrying about our problems. The dog is making an exciting adventure out of his familiar walk while we hardly notice it. We're not really there, worrying about the past or future. Yet all this can be turned around to our advantage.

It's very doubtful that a dog can sit in its basket and think, 'Isn't it quite extraordinary that here I sit, a four-legged animal in the house of the strange human creature who, instead of eating me, feeds me pieces of other animals and generally looks after me as if I were a human baby.'

Awareness! The same mind that can destroy the present and replace it with a future which may never happen can, however, also bring the Now to vivid life and enhance the present. 'Here I am,' an enlightened Kahuna might think. 'Three souls in a physical body which is trotting across Pooh Park, followed by this strange little four-legged animal which has somehow turned human beings into a friend. I must enjoy this moment as much as my dog friend as nothing lasts forever.'

You have rewritten your autobiography. Nothing is easier to forget than our advantages in life—which young person under the delusion that youth lasts forever, is grateful for being young?—and nothing is harder to forget than our disadvantages. You no longer make this oh-so-human mistake and regularly list the good things in your life if you've got nothing better to do. The sense of being lucky gives your *life-illusion* (to use John Cowper Powys' happy phrase meaning your concept of yourself) a feel-good factor. You know you're lucky, your JO has a happy inner glow and you regularly feel him or her a dollop of feel-good news every now and then. JO's optimism has improved your health and energy. Life is good.

What the heck did I use to moan about in the pre-Kahuna days? Our troubles can become just as phantasmal as the good things of life we have been ignoring for so long.

When problems arise you hit them with the power of positive thought. Positive thought is already out and about in the land. I was very impressed by seeing a young black guy on TV who lost a leg in the London 7/7 bombings—to make matters worse he had been a dancer if I remember correctly. When asked if he hated the bombers he replied he didn't because he didn't want them to play any further part in his life. He'd just mentally obliterated them with a positive choice to carry on with life. I hope you don't have to make any such heroic positive choices in your life, positive reader, but this guy showed what can be done in horrible circumstances.

You have also introduced the sacred power of creativity into your life, a power vividly and innocently witnessed in children's paintings, for example. Incidentally, some educationalists want to replace this delightful flowering with stale academic tricks while children's creativity is under threat from time-consuming video games. You, creative reader, have seen the light, and, whether it's a painting or a project, you go to sleep content and wake up in the morning knowing that it, the great project, the guiding light, has mysteriously developed while you were asleep!

The next step from this happy state of affairs is magic and the agent of magic is vital force. Vital force is an extraordinarily versatile energy which the emerald tablet suggests played a part in the creation of the world. All psychic phenomena involves vital force which can both transmit ideas or teleport objects. In psychic surgery vital force cuts flesh like a laser beam, spoons are bent with vital force while in genuine fire walking it insulates the feet from harm. I have a hunch that the anomalies of quantum physics are caused by the fact that scientists are investigating electrons which are so small that they involve the paradoxes of vital force.

Although, as we shall see, the phenomenon is frequently demonstrated, our scientists would never dare to acknowledge its existence. If any of them were open-minded enough to do so they would instantly lose all credibility, be blacklisted and become scientific non-persons as a recent BBC documentary called 'Heroes' revealed. Oh for the enlightened Victorian era when a distinguished scientist such as Sir William Crookes could investigate spiritualism without fear of being rubbed out of scientific history!

TWO
VITAL FORCE

The rain that slides down from its source, and ebbs back subtly, with a strange energy generated between its coming and going, an energy which, even to our science, is of life; this man has to conquer . . . The Indian, like the old Egyptian, seeks to make the conquest from the mystic will within him, pitted against the Cosmic Dragon
D. H. Lawrence, 'Mornings is Mexico'

So far we have dealt with easily grasped concepts—the Low Self and the Middle Self which resemble the unconscious and ego of popular Freudianism (although, as we have seen, JO who has been mistakenly labelled by Mr Freud as the 'unconscious' is an all too conscious self). By a little simple self-examination we can see how JO helps the rational Myself in every area of life, from memory to skills, and is also the emotional powerhouse of humanity. On the other hand, we realise how JO needs the guidance of the Middle Self to co-exist with other human beings. Only dictators or rock stars can live in society without curbing JO and even the mighty are eventually called to account—by their own failing overindulged bodies if nothing else.

The Low Self is not only an emotional powerhouse, however, for it also transmits and generates an energy which our scientists stubbornly refuse to acknowledge—rather as they refuse to recognise the existence of soul or even mind. Max Freedom Long called this energy vital force.

What is vital force?

Lawrence, though he never declared an interest in magic, was in fact a psychic and the above quote from *Mornings in Mexico* can refer only to vital force. Lawrence's preternaturally sensitive vision enables him to describe vital force rising like a blue flame from, say, the stallion St Mawr or actual Mexican children playing. In the above passage from Lawrence the only false note, stemming perhaps from his own wilful aggression, is the use of the word 'conquest'; the Kahunas worked *with* the cosmic dragon rather than conquering it.

Vital force is, in fact, not an obscure energy but something we are already familiar with though we don't give it a name. This is due to the grotesque materialism of Western science and the white-coated devils' stubborn refusal to acknowledge what he can't understand and doesn't want to acknowledge anyway. Vital force is known as *chi* in China, *ki* in Japan and *prana* in India. It is the *astral light* mentioned in occult writings.

It's a miserable grey winter's day. Life seems to have ground to a halt in some hopeless, foggy, suburban cul-de-sac. It is all over for us . . . And then the sun breaks through the clouds. Instantly, all is changed. The world has become not only a brighter but also a more hopeful place. It's hard to recall the mood of despair we experienced only a few minutes ago. This is because the sun is not just an electric bulb in the sky but a powerhouse of vital force and this vital force instantly lifts our spirits. Mystics know that the rising and setting sun contains concentrated vital force and make their prayers in these conditions accordingly.

Suppose the sun doesn't shine. It's still that grey day at the end of the cul-de-sac. But then the telephone rings with good news. It's the hospital and you haven't got it. Or it's the man you fancy ringing up. Or it's the national lottery and you have won. Suddenly, whereas before you were dragging your weary self along like a wounded snake, now your spirits are soaring like a supercharged eagle. You dance! You could run a mile!

This is because we can generate our own vital force by converting the body's blood sugars into this energy.

Have you ever desperately, desperately, desperately needed extra strength and speed? If you're a man it might be when—guess what?—you're attacked in the street. Or let's say you're on an idyllic country walk when, you disturb a wild wasp nest and you find yourself surrounded by buzzing wasps. Or, if you're a mother you've taken your eye off the toddler for a second to open the hamper and he's gone and fallen into the river. In such fraught situations you acquire a bear-like strength or miraculous agility and you fly over fences and across country with a speed you would have previously considered impossible or, as if fired from a cannon, you plunge into the river and rescue little one.

These miracles of strength and speed are achieved because you've been supercharged with vital force. Women lift up cars to rescue their babies, men rip doors off burning jeeps to rescue someone inside and Ernest Hemingway, that remarkably accident-prone man, smashed his way out of a burning aircraft with his head. The great actor Rod Steiger was tone deaf and couldn't sing a note. Hope lives eternal in the human breast, however, and this didn't stop him, having been in the movie, from auditioning for the stage show of 'Oklahoma'. "If there's a cancer," said Rogers to Hammerstein upon hearing Steiger's ghastly squawks. "You've got to cut it out." Steiger was so incandescent with rage at being fired from the show that he crashed through the locked, steel-reinforced EXIT door *without damaging his shoulder.*

How did Tina Turner blow up such a storm? She said she could talk all day about the mysterious energy which she generated in performance. She was once limp with glandular fever and had to record a TV show and the energy miraculously flooded back once she was on stage. Another diva, Edith Piaf, was crippled with arthritis and the only time her claw-like hands could open was when she was on stage giving her all.

So far we've been describing the natural use of vital force, how it comes with sunlight, with good news, floods us in an emergency—or is intuitively employed by extraordinary people such as Tina or Elvis. Some of the above examples of vital force, say Steiger's assault on the steel door, would defy scientific explanation.

There is a long tradition of increasing the power of vital force by breath control. (In fact, the root meaning of spirit is the Latin word *spiritus* meaning 'a breath' from *spiro* 'to breathe'.)

The association of vital force with breath became plain silly with the Chinese Dauist philosophy. The Chinese quite properly recognised Chi (vital force) but at one point in their history they totally confused vital force with breath. They believed that you were given a finite amount of vital force breath at birth and, if you lost that vital breath, you sickened and died which made wind problems a deadly liability. Never eat beans or you could blow yourself away. The precious vital force breath could even be lost after you had died, as well as in life, and your soul might be caught short of vital force needed to help it out of the corpse. Hence corpses had their orifices plugged up lest a vital breath of life should escape too soon.

The Low Self of a Chinese Dauist who violently farted might well have concluded that all was lost, logged off the health computer and caused serious illness if not death. Thus can a practical recognition of vital force drift into absurdity. Psychic and religious affairs are rife with this sort of misunderstanding.

The enhancement of vital force by breath control is known as pranayama in the East. I have no doubt that yogic practitioners achieve wonders with breathing exercises though it hasn't worked for myself. Paul Brunton, a wonderful philosopher writing about these problems, believed that pranayama is unsuitable for Westerners and just causes them breathing problems. Max Freedom Long declared that Eastern breath exercises were over complicated and that all that was needed was a few deep breaths to recharge your vital force.

The jury is out as far as I am concerned.

Vital force in the hands of an adept is extraordinary and defies modern science (which is why the white-coated devil chooses not to investigate it). Those who collapse after being touched on the forehead by the revivalist preacher (assuming it's not a setup) have been harmlessly stunned by vital force which may heal them when they come to. You're likely to see this sort of demonstration on TV if you haven't seen it in person. According to Max Freedom Long the Kahunas could charge up sticks with stun vital force and the largest brave would faint if hit by one.

Fig 4. WHAT MAKES THE LADY SO STRONG?

In the 11th card of the Tarot she opens the jaws of a lion. Note she is wearing a hat twisted in the infinity sign ∞, the emniscate, and the sign of the High Self.

Awesome demonstrations of vital force are out there on TV. A Ukrainian medium appeared on TV in the Paul McKenna (A famous UK hypnotist) Show in 1996. This man threaded wires through his flesh underneath his biceps and pulled a freight wagon along the tracks with these wires. He was neither panting nor in pain at the end of this performance. On the Chris Tarrant (a famous UK quizmaster) Show a Buddhist monk bounced a huge log swinging from the rafters, heavy enough to smash down a reinforced door, off his naked abdomen. The reaction of the studio audience watching the video was significant—conditioned by Western science and unable to understand what they were seeing *they roared with laughter.*

When you have a society which is totally ignorant of spiritual forces a huge communication gap arises. Wretched magicians widen the gap further with their bewildering antics which confuse psychic phenomena with trickery.

Recently in 2005 there's been a fascinating TV series called 'Spirit, Body and Kick Ass Moves' hosted by a martial arts expert called Chris Crudelli. He has featured some amazing feats of strength powered by vital force. One Chinese guy pulled a Transit van by a chain attached to his (ouch!) penis while other Chinese bounced razor-sharp swords off their bellies. One adept (Ugh!) bent an iron bar by pressing it against the ground with his *eyeball!* Of course, no white-coated devil would even dare to investigate such phenomena for if he did the scientific establishment would see to it that he was no longer regarded as a serious scientist.

Alas, boys will be boys, and they will weaponise anything—including vital force. One middle-aged Chinese expert could inject deadly vital force, a vital force which could injure or even kill, with the palm of his hand at some distance from his victims. Chris Crudelli bravely took a shot of it and was in serious discomfort. The lethal expert had to drive it out with a slap on the back, rather like winding a child, before he recovered.

Personally, I am aware of vital force rising through my feet when I am healing people. I can direct it around my body. Once I met a fellow healer who grasped my hand and said, "Feel this." Sure enough I could feel his vital force travelling through his hand coolly up to my elbow. "And you feel this," I said, pushing his vital force out of my arm into his body, much to his surprise. Healers become competitive over vital force.

Healing vital force can be sent through an astonishing psychic 'internet' and I, as an agent of higher forces, can send vital force to anyone anywhere in the world. When my daughter put her back out on Bondi Beach in Australia I sent energy to her. Contact was almost instantaneous and I could feel a strange throbbing as if I was contacting her through the earth's field. Her back soon recovered. You could write an entire book about vital force. Teams of scientists should be employed studying it.

Unfortunately, those scientists who have investigated vital force—or a related power—scientists such as Viktor Schauberger or Wilhelm Reich, have been ignored or even imprisoned. Wilhelm Reich was originally a disciple of Freud's but when Freud announced that the unconscious was essentially destructive, Reich quite properly realised that psychoanalysis had failed.

Freud, observing such phenomena as the Nazi party and the history of warfare, understandably but mistakenly concluded that humanity has a death wish. As we have seen, the atrocities human beings regularly commit are frequently social atrocities. Which brave and nice young Englishman on holiday would of his own volition explode depleted uranium on the unfortunate people of Iraq? As a member of the RAF under the command of Tony Blair such an atrocity can be committed, however, with a more or less clear conscience. 'Doing me job' or 'Defending me country' or 'Obeying orders'.

Reich didn't believe in the culpability of the entire human race and he was also worried that psychoanalysis was too expensive for the working class and sought a quicker solution to peoples' problems.

Believing that mental problems were caused by the blocked energies of sexual failure and muscular armouring, Reich investigated the energy released at orgasm but, as his researches deepened, found himself analysing the life force itself. He called vital force orgone energy and also detected deadly orgone or DOR, the reverse of life force. According to Reich, when you look at a blue sky you are looking through the miles of orgone which creates the blueness of the earth's mantle. He created the orgone accumulator (a simple box structure in which you could sit) to capture orgone and the cloud buster, a device looking like a multiple rocket launcher (featured in a Kate Bush video with Donald Sutherland as Reich) which acted as a sort of lightning conductor to draw down DOR energy from the sky. Having become an enemy of Freud, an enemy of the Nazis, Reich became an enemy of the European communists. He left Europe to set up shop in America, where the poor man finally became the enemy of American capitalism and, imprisoned for contempt of court, had his books burnt and died in prison. Madman or genius? A guy who makes so many enemies must have something going for him!

It seems that the Western world is unwilling to recognise vital force even when it is scientifically demonstrated.

Max Freedom Long discovered that vital force is the energy which powers the Kahuna system—not to mention the entire universe. Vital force is not some spooky juice created by magicians but pervades our world; without this life force everything would just wither and die.

One of the Kahuna symbols for vital force is water as Lawrence intuitively realised. Now water is a universal substance, permeating the atmosphere in vapour form, pouring down in rain, filling up ponds, leaking away and rising heavenwards again in the form of vapour. Like water vital force is everywhere, can pour down, fill up, leak away and ascend. Pressurised water can be extremely powerful—as can concentrated vital force. The psychic phenomena of table turning, powered by vital force, was popular in Victorian England; when strong men attempted to hold down a levitating table it proved to be impossible to do so.

Unlike water, however, vital force can be directed by the human mind. Indeed, it's the link between mind and matter. Philosophers in the nineteenth century became so hypnotized by the supposed differences between mind and matter that they just couldn't understand how mind could actually influence matter. 'How on earth can a mental wish to raise one's arm make that material arm rise up?' these clever philosophical boobies asked themselves endlessly. Vital force, you dummies.

And could this rising and falling, ebbing and flowing ambience of vital force be directed by the will of humankind and made to work for us thanks to Kahuna science?

Max Freedom Long believed it could.

Exercise 16
Sensing vital force

Let's see if you how sensitive you are to vital force.

(a) Rub the palms of your hands and place them facing each other as if holding an invisible ball.
(b) Now. What do you feel on the palms of your hands? If you feel a tenuous balloon of tingling energy then you are sensitive to the vital force which is the stuff resonating between your palms. If you don't feel it then it's still there.
(c) Keeping your hands a foot from your body, run those sensitive palms around your head, your trunk, and your legs. Do you feel any difference in the vital force, a 'hot spot' where you have a dodgy knee say? If you can then you can detect signs of disease.
(d) Have a go at sensing each other's vital force with a friend.
(e) Sense the energies given off by computers and mobile phones. Personally I don't like being in the same room as an activated cell phone.

THREE
VITAL FORCE AND HYPNOSIS—CUTTING OUT THE MIDDLE MAN

A subject lying flat on the floor is put into a trance and instructed by the hypnotist that their body is now a steel girder. Lo and behold, the subject can be lifted, stretched between two chairs and heavy men can now stand on the subject's stomach as if flesh has indeed been transformed into a beam.

What has happened to the body of an ordinary member of the public who has foolishly agreed to be a stage hypnotist's subject?

What happens is that the rational Middle Self is no longer in charge of the window of consciousness. It's no good the hypnotist telling a wide-awake Middle Self that our body is going to be transformed into a girder because we won't believe it for a single second. 'Of course, it can't be,' we would say. 'It's quite impossible.'

The hypnotist's 'Watch this little swinging pendulum . . . Your eyes are getting heavy' patter is to send the sceptical Middle Self onto the mind's back burner. Hypnotised subjects sometimes report that their Middle Self can observe what's happening as if from a nearby psychic room but is unable to prevent it. The first job of the hypnotist, of course, is to find suggestible people who are easily hypnotised. Having established that someone is a good hypnotic subject and put them into a trance once, the hypnotist merely has to touch them in future, imparting a little vital force, to send them into a trance again and have a direct line to their Low Self. Hypnosis demonstrates both the frightening power and equally frightening vulnerability of JO.

"You are a steel girder," says the hypnotist.

"I'm a steel girder?" says JO. "All right then." The Low Self then draws in that amazingly versatile vital force power to the spirit body, concentrates it and transforms the body itself into a girder of sorts.

Does vital force have limits in protecting the body? The awesome demonstrations of vital force in insulating the body against razor sharp swords doesn't mean it can stop a bullet. During the Boxer Rebellion to overthrow British Victorian colonial rule the Chinese rebels, led astray by demonstrations of the power of vital force, were convinced that British bullets would bounce off them. They didn't.

When you see hypnosis in action, an awesome demonstration of mind over matter, the ability of JO to cure or cause physical illness doesn't seem at all improbable.

The post-hypnotic suggestion state—whereby the subject, having apparently woken from the trance and being restored to normality is still under the hypnotist's control—is a worrying phenomenon if we entertain any belief in the independence of the human mind.

"Now," says the hypnotist making a post-hypnotic suggestion while the subject is still in a trance state. "You will wake up but when I snap my fingers you will be Mick Jagger with arthritis singing 'Jumping Jack Flash'." And, sure enough, some previously shy member of the public is soon outdoing Rory Bremner in a hilarious performance.

Of course, talented JO, the Low Self, instead of merely lurking in the background of the personality as normal, is now being dragged out onto an actual stage to entertain an audience of real people. This can cause problems for what is a naturally retiring soul whose normal playground is the world of dreams. Perhaps the Low Self might enjoy its outing and want to take charge again in the real world—and we know that JO is a thoroughly unsatisfactory leader. Some hypnotic subjects who've allowed a sleazy hypnotist to make them clown about on stage have flashback incidents.

Another aspect of post-hypnotic suggestion, apart from demonstrating the astounding show-business skills latent in the 'ordinary' person, reveals just how tenuous our grasp of reality can be. "Now," said hypnotist Paul McKenna to a hypnotised subject, "When I snap my fingers you will wake but I will be completely invisible to you." Snaps his fingers and the subject wakes up and behaves as if normal. When the hypnotist raises a glass in front of the subject, however, as McKenna is now invisible, the post-hypnotic subject is terrified of the levitating glass.

Everyday life frequently puts us in a trance-like condition. Sit in a stationary car and pretend to 'drive' it for three hours. You'd go mad. But you're quite capable of really driving for hours on a motorway. Stare

Joe Potts

at a wall for three hours and you'd go mad. You can stare at the TV for three hours with no trouble at all, however, because both driving and TV watching involve trance-like conditions.

And are we in a political trance? Mrs Thatcher, for example, internationalised the UK while posing as a nationalist but her nationalist voters didn't seem to notice the reality of what was happening. In dreams the Fat Man from Fartland who is about to blow away the earth can terrify JO. Ridiculous isn't it? Yet post-hypnotic suggestion reveals that ridiculous beliefs can be planted in hypnotised JO and flower in the Middle Self in a full waking state.

Perhaps we ought to have a reality check occasionally and observe what strange notions we've innocently taken on board.

Can we hypnotize ourselves?

We do it all the time.

Take mum. How is it that she puts up with Little Snot, a demanding, grizzling, manic toddler with a cry to tear sheet metal in half who somehow thinks he's as worthy of attention as Elvis himself? He wants to jump in front of the traffic! He wants to rot his teeth with endless gobstoppers! He wants to get his greedy, sticky mitts on every imitation weapon produced by the toy trade! He beats the cat with a plastic sword and fires air balls into mum's face! Why hasn't she just let him jump in front of a passing pantechnicon? How can she lead him about with a (taut) smile on her face and day things like, "No, darling, you've already got a Nerg Laser Zapper."

Because she's hypnotised herself into being A Mother. 'I've brought this beast who I love really into the world.' She's tells herself. 'I'm a mother and a mother I will remain no matter how much it hurts.'

Cars, TVs, politicians, admen, lovers and even open fires can all hypnotise us.

And like the long-suffering mum we can hypnotize ourselves. How easy is it? Will 'Day by day and in everyway I am getting better and better' self-hypnotize us into good health?

The problem lies with Myself the Clever One. A hypnotist has to put the Middle Self onto the back burner to plug into JO down there. The mum has Nature telling her to be A Mother as well as making her own self-denying choice.

If our Middle Self says, 'I'm going to turn my arm into an iron bar but I don't think this is really going to work' then you can't expect the listening JO to obligingly concentrate the vital force and do the job.

Self-hypnosis will only work if reasoning you is utterly convinced it will work. You've got to believe it will happen—unless you've got a gift and it just happens naturally. I suspect that all adepts start with a certain aptitude—just as an electrician is naturally immune to the sort of electric shocks which would put most of us off the trade immediately.

Max found that fire-eaters had always had a friendly relationship with fire before they learned how to control it.

Apparently you learn how to control fire by staring and staring and staring at candle flame . . . until you understand *the soul of the flame*.

Viktor Schauberger—forester, mystic and scientist—said you can do the same with water, that you could let part of your soul drift away with the river and it would return with knowledge of the soul of water.

Exercise 17
Magnetic movement

The actor Burt Lancaster, declaring he would kill a certain film producer, vaulted over a sofa towards his prey. His victim was rooted to the spot, hypnotised by the sheer beauty of Lancaster's movements. Lancaster is a perfect example of magnetic movement, movement stately yet empowered with vital force.

Learn magnetic movement

(a) Close your fist.
(b) Signal to your open hand that you are about to close your fist. But don't close it. You will feel the vital force that was going to close your fist tingling in your hand.
(c) Slowly but purposefully close your fist as if gently squeezing a sponge of vital force. This is a magnetic movement.
(d) Raise your arms above your head as if they are floating on vital force.

(e) Aikido is a form of martial arts using, as the name suggests, vital force and, whereas karate practitioners become increasingly stiff and battered as time goes by, Aikido experts who can perform such feats as making their body impregnable to blows remain remarkably sprightly.

(f) Tai Chi is supposed to be performed, not just in slow-mo, but with magnetic movement.

FOUR
THINGS GET COMPLICATED

> *"That which is above is like to that which is below, and that which is below is like to that which is above, to accomplish the miracles of one thing."*
> The Emerald tablet of Hermes Trismigistus

Though this famous sentence is often taken to mean that the planets above influence our destiny below on earth I believe it can also mean that the energy of the High Self is related to the energy of the Low Self, that the High Self can feed off JO's animal energies to transform physical reality. This dynamic of vital force can involve the Middle Self of an adept when the High Self is contacted *deliberately,* although, as we've seen, in an emergency the Low Self can sometimes contact the High Self and create, say, miraculous strength without the Middle Self having any idea of what's really happening.

So far, dedicated reader, you've taken on board the concept of Me, Myself and I and the miracles which can spontaneously or deliberately occur when the three interact.

Let's have a look at the idea of a spirit body.

Everything is a vibration as the opera singer breaking the glass demonstrates. The opera singer's voice vibrates at the same frequency as the glass, stretches that frequency and shatters the glass. Resonance science which can be used to destroy diseases or, according to that dangerous genius Nikola Tesla, even split the earth in half, is a hugely important field of study and some of Tesla's resonance theories have been incorporated into engineering.

It is all a question of frequency of vibration. Light waves are called waves because they behave like waves across a pond after a stone has been thrown in it—as do all the waves of the electromagnetic spectrum which covers everything from microwaves, to light waves, to radioactive waves (but not waves of vital force as yet). What differentiates these waves is their frequency or the speed at which they vibrate. Change their frequency and these waves of energy become radio waves, light waves, killer radiation waves or high-frequency healing waves. It's highly confusing to us non-scientific members of the public who regard radio waves, say, as a totally different order of energy from light and then find that ingenious scientists—and there was none more ingenious than Nikola Tesla who invented an AC/DC current machine when all scientists declared this to be impossible—are manipulating the basic stuff of energy into electricity or radio waves like magicians. If we are non-scientists we receive their inventions as native people received beads from traders.

Similarly a spirit body is distinguished from a physical body, by occupying a different etheric vibration. Mind and matter, like light and radioactivity, are at different places *on the same spectrum.* If the soul belonged to a different energy spectrum to the body it couldn't inhabit and control the body. Alternative writings claim that a sinister technology already exists which can draw the soul out of the body and who knows? Such matters are obscured with disinformation and perhaps we'll never know the truth.

There has, however, been confirmation of the existence of spirit bodies by Kirlian photography, a photographic method whereby the plate itself is electrified and records etheric energies from something pressed against it. Experiments have shown that, if you tear a leaf in half and then photograph it with the Kirlian technique, you will produce a photograph of the *whole* leaf, the spirit body of the leaf, which will remain intact while half the physical leaf has been removed. The spirit half will eventually fade until only the surviving physical half can be photographed. Kirlian photography can also record the large amount of vital force given off by a healer's hand.

Max Freedom Long discovered that we have three souls, three spirit bodies for these souls and three different energies for these souls. It's now getting rather complicated. The Low Self and the Middle Self souls live *in* the body whereas the High Self exists on the top of or *above* the head, symbolised by a halo in some old religious paintings.

The Low Self has a strange spirit body. When Max the great researcher was investigating the meanings of the *unihipili*, the Low Self, one of the most puzzling root syllables of the word was *pili*—which means 'sticky, acting as a servant, a spirit which *sticks to another*'. The 'servant' meaning and the sticking to another refers to the relationship of the Low to the

Middle Self, as the reader already knows. The meaning of *pili*, after Max had teased out the full implications, are surprising indeed. The etheric body of JO is made of shadowy body substance, the 'aka' body, which *sticks and clings and cleaves to everything which the conscious mind comes into contact with* and, having stuck, draws itself out in an enduring psychic thread. So that we are connected for all our lives with every person we meet and everything we touch in a myriad web of sticky threads like a tangle drawn from psychic glue.

The tribal chieftain, (ignorant savage according to the white-coated devil) while being carried aloft in his chair, accompanied by a invigorating rumble of drums perhaps, enjoyed nothing so much as a good, if dangerous, spit into the dirt. An important member of his team, the royal gob-catcher, would then hastily retrieve this spittle because it was a threat to his boss to leave it lying there. As it came from the chieftain's body an *aka* thread would lead back from the spittle to the big man's spirit. Just suppose a hostile sorcerer got hold of that spittle; he could put a curse on it and the dark charge would surge along the *aka* thread into the chieftain's spirit and send him into rapid decline.

Nail or hair clippings, any bodily detritus, carried a similar risk and could not be left lying around. The authorities are now desirous of capturing our spittle—for the DNA it contains.

It was risky to even let your real name be known in case the sorcerer got his hands on that. Your real name was therefore a closely guarded secret. Having a secret name for your JO, incidentally, is quite a good idea; it could stop you being hypnotized. It's no use the hypnotist saying, "You're going to sleep, Kylie" if your real, secret JO name is Boudicca.

The Low Self can project a sticky finger to someone's spirit body to read their mind. Thus if you feel 'He says the right things but there's something odd about this man' it could be your JO which has brought you the information. The Low Self also has the vital task of sending energy to the High Self along an *aka* thread.

So all the traditional stuff about suppressing the animal in yourself and crushing your desires to achieve spirituality is very bad advice indeed. Suppress the animal side of your being and you wreck the trinity of mind.

Guilt is the big showstopper!

To the Kahunas guilt was known as the log across the path preventing psychic healing or development. The Low Self plays a vital role in the trinity of mind. Despite being irrational and hysterical JO generates the low voltage vital force which the Kahunas called *mana*. The Low Self is the boiler room for the trinity of mind. If the Low Self has been made to feel unworthy through guilt then he or she is in no state to wholeheartedly generate the vital force needed for psychic activity. Hence the ritual of bringing gifts to the God to be contacted or, in a modern context, giving a painful sum to charity. This is to make the supplicant feel good about themselves, thus banishing the dead weight of guilt.

The Low Self manufactures the vital force for all three selves.

How does the Middle Self figure in all this? The Clever One can produce little vital force on its own. It's no good asking for healing energy to course through your hands if you haven't the co-operation of the Low Self and the High Self. The Middle Self, which we tend to think of as us, our soul, is totally dependent on JO down there when it comes to vital force. What part does the Middle Self actually play in psychic activities then?

The Middle Self adds the *power of will* to the *mana* of the Low Self which becomes *manamana*. Max teased out two different meanings of this term. One means that this is shared or divided energy, the Low Self sharing it with the Middle Self. The other meaning is to branch out and move upward or outward as *a growing vine.*

The vine climbs upwards bearing grapes, grapes which represent *clusters of thought forms.* Vital force is an energy which can carry ideas!

The Middle Self, then, by means of choice and will can send energised ideas to the Aumakua, the High Self. The High Self then profoundly changes the *manamana* energy to *mana loa*, the miraculous, atom-smashing energy. This is the highest form of energy, the energy that enables healing, for example, to take place.

The beautiful Egyptian stele of the Lady Tuth Shena (see book cover) has been the subject of various interpretations, most of which are recognised to be thoroughly dubious. The best an academic can come up with is that she is sunbathing and that the flowers of energy represent sunlight. No one really knows what the image is about. The lady, standing before a little table of offerings, is pointing the palms of her hands towards Horus, a bird-headed god. Birds are creatures of the heavens and represent higher spirituality and therefore a man with a bird's head is a higher being. From the disc above the head of Horus stream lines of flower heads towards the lady.

To a healer who has read Max Freedom Long the meaning of the image is perfectly obvious.

Raising the palms of the hands is a means of sending or receiving vital force. In absent healing, for example, as far as I am concerned, both happen. I can feel the vibrations of a patient on my palms as soon as I think of the patient and raise my hands. Apart from receiving their vibration I am also sending healing energy. Sometimes the results of absent healing are dramatic (one lady who I was talking to on the phone went in a trance and chanted in a strange Celtic language) though hands-on healing in person is much more effective in my own case.

One of the charming features of Egyptian art is that it reveals a culture very much aware of subtle energies. People of all classes, from the Pharaoh downwards, are frequently to be seen making the healing gesture with outstretched palms which can sense, send or receive vital force.

In this context the meaning of the image is plain; it's an almost a textbook illustration of Kahuna theory. The lady, after making her offerings of bread and fruit to the god as Max advises, has sent a prayer wrapped in vital force through her hands to Horus. The god's High Self, represented by the disc above the head, has heightened the energy and is sending her back blossoming *mana loa* pictured appropriately as a stream of flowers.

Ten elements—three souls, three spirit bodies, three energies enclosed in the physical body—makes for a complicated picture and I found Max's diagram rather unsatisfactory. Help came from a strange quarter as we shall see in the next chapter. Incidentally, enthusiastic reader, I believe the interaction of vital force in the Trinity of Mind is a field still wide-open to further research and you yourself may well discover some further information to add to this fascinating and vitally important subject.

Joe Potts

Fig 5. THE STELE OF THE LADY TUTH SHEA
Sending a prayer to the A*umakua* of Horus and receiving *mana loa*.

FIVE
THE MIND FIELD

I wondered if I could produce a better diagram than Max to illustrate the ten elements of the Kahunas system. Help came from an unexpected source.

Crop circles are a phenomenon which has attracted as much disinformation as psychic phenomena itself. The glyphs have an abstract beauty which puts to shame fifty years of abstract art, have inspired mathematicians and scientists, are filled with a mysterious radiation (vital force perhaps?), contain genetically-altered seeds and are laid down without the crop being snapped. Yet it is widely believed that a sinister pair of hicks, Doug and Dave, created these marvels after staggering out of the pub at night with planks. The passing of these two has not dispelled the absurd belief that the duo offer an explanation of the crop circle phenomena, despite the fact that astonishing designs continue to appear long after their demise.

I was wondering if I could think of a diagram to represent the complex Kahuna system when, to my delight, I came across a famous crop circle. This extraordinary pictogram appeared overnight with a rumble of thunder and the flashing of mysterious lights below the hill fort at Barbury Castle on the 16th July 1991. This crop circle opened a new era in design. Hitherto, crop glyphs, which had begun as circles, had produced images suggestive of stone-age cultures, cup and ring patterns and such like.

The Barbury Castle pictogram was a leap into complex geometry and put an end to ludicrous scientific theories that crop circles were caused by the wind, a mini-tornado perhaps. The pictogram, perfectly laid down in the wheat and covering a total area of 10,000 metres, became known in the British press as 'the Mother of all Pictograms'—though even this amazing design has often been surpassed many times in complexity and size over the years.

Fig 6. THE KAHUNA SYSTEM AS ILLUSTRATED BY THE BARBARY CASTLE CROP CIRCLE

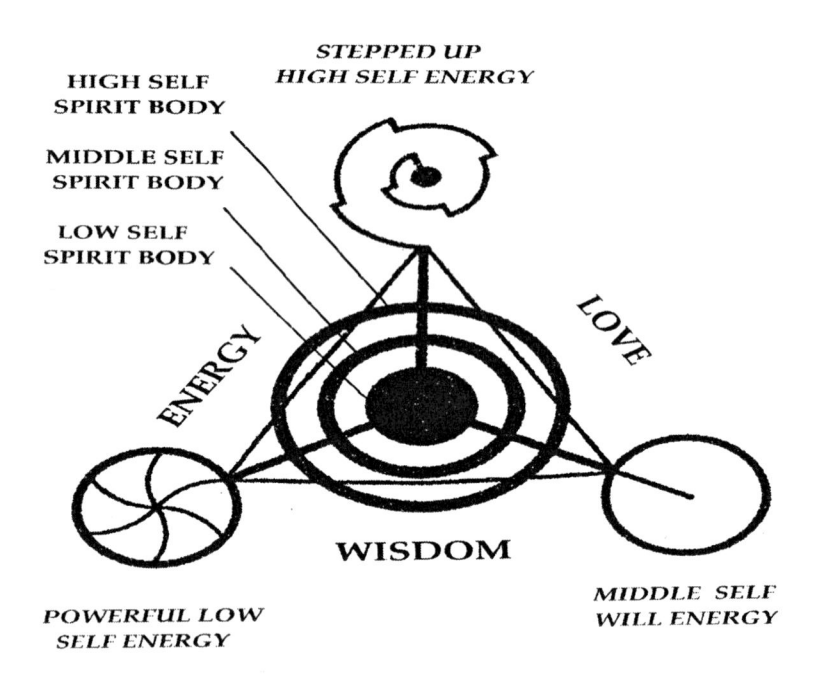

Astonishingly, the pictogram gives a well-nigh perfect diagram for the representation of nine of the elements involved in Kahuna magic. Coincidence or communication from the stars? Who cares? It works.

Here we have the three souls represented by the three sides of the equilateral triangle, that ancient sacred symbol of the trinity. I've called them love, wisdom and energy to represent the High, Middle and Low Self respectively.

Three spirit bodies for the three souls are represented by two circles and an infilled circle—the big, fat, dot is suggestive of the Low Self's involvement with the material world. The circle after the black circle represents the Middle Self spirit body and the biggest circle of all is half in and half out of the triangle—just as the High Self can be half in and half out of the body.

The three energies of the three selves are represented by the symbols on the apexes of the triangle. The Low Self circle is full of vigorous lines of energy while the Middle Self circle is empty as it has only the energy of will. The High Self energy can generate, to use Max Freedom Long's expression, *'stepped up'*, atom-smashing energy and here are the steps.

Connect them all up, let the whole represent the human body containing the system and 'the mother of all pictograms' gives us a diagram of the Kahuna system as neat as the London underground map.

It is an excellent guide for making puzzling psychic phenomena easy to understand at a glance. For example, those mysterious cases where we get a sombre warning, sometimes accompanied by that sinking feeling, not to overtake that car or to cancel the plane booking. "I just got this terrible sinking feeling about the holiday in Florida and cancelled the whole thing or I'd have been on the plane that disappeared into the Atlantic."

Warnings like this are sent by the Aumakua, sometimes known as the Guardian Angel, which can see into the future and which sends information to the other selves. JO receives the message with feelings of foreboding but it's up to the Middle Self to recognise the warning and act accordingly. Being unaware of or ignoring our intuitive faculties can be dangerous and expensive business. Modern life has blunted our intuition. In the South Sea Islands, Kahuna territory, Robert Louis Stevenson discovered that telepathy was *the* means of communication and news also passed telepathically from one side of the island to another faster than word of mouth.

He met a man who knew telepathically his brother was going to return home that day on a ship making a rare visit to the island even though he'd had no letters from him for years.

'Atom-busting' healing can only be channelled through the High Self whereas Low Self can only send a much more limited form of healing energy. Gurdjieff once passed restorative energy to a follower who was feeling dead with exhaustion at the end of World War II. When the acolyte, now feeling better, looked at Gurdjieff, however, the guru had aged ten years! He had used up his own energy whereas a real healer channels energy *through* himself from the High Self and can heal frequently without being tired. I used heal several people in a row unless I'd got a bug hanging round.

If the healer's vital force consists only of Low Self energy and isn't the *stepped up* energy created by the High Self there just won't be any miraculous healing, just possibly a temporary improvement in the patient's condition.

SIX
DOWSING

When you say, "Give me *yes*, pendulum" and the pendulum obligingly swings clockwise like magic it is tempting in the first flush of excitement to get carried away and ask all sorts of questions—such as what the winning lottery number is going to be. Dowsers sometimes suggest that it's immoral to ask the pendulum for financial help. Personally, I can't see why. Money is the lifeblood of society and if we need a large transfusion why shouldn't we ask for it? Sometimes we English, even at this late date, can be too self-effacing for our own good.

Max Freedom Long got help from the Kahunas to sell his photographic business, which was a financial transaction after all, and devote himself to writing those invaluable books.

Uri Geller did report a bad experience from the Powers Above when he asked for help in a gambling matter (he seemed to be virtually thrown out of his taxi by invisible forces) but then he went dowsing oil and minerals for big companies, a much more environmentally destructive activity, and wasn't psychically punished at all. He himself can't see that logic of the situation and neither can I.

Let's be quite clear. The pendulum is almost certainly being swung by the Low Self which controls the involuntary movements of the body to make it swing. It's unlikely on your first attempt that it's going to come up with the correct lottery number or answer any big questions in your life.

However, just as some dreams are a surreal Low Self jumble and some dreams channel information from the High Self (Predicting the future and solving creative problems), some pendulum findings are the work of the Low Self while *some channel information from the High Self itself.* Thus some gifted dowsers can come up with miraculous information. I know a woman who can dowse your health in detail and suggest remedies after being sent a piece of hair, for example. Some dowsers can successfully dowse for water over *a map of unfamiliar territory.* Clearly the Low Self isn't picking up any actual vibrations given off by an underground stream while dowsing over a sheet of paper. Only if the High Self is providing the Low Self with information can this miraculous dowsing occur. As the Aumakua is in touch with the World Mind and the Akashic Records, it is able to access all knowledge and locating underground water or oil from a previously unseen map is no problem.

Dowsing actual water beneath the ground is JO at work because the Low Self is sensitive to the subtle vibrations given off, say, by an underground water pipe and can process sensitive information most people aren't aware of.

In my own case, I am so sensitive to a variety of subtle energies which I can feel tingling on my hands so that I hardly need a pendulum or dowsing rod to discover what's going on beneath me. On the other hand, despite having joined dowsing clubs and with the best will in the world, I have not as yet developed my dowsing abilities to channel High Self information. When I have a go at the tests on dowsing practice day, for example, I cannot find that glass of water with salt in it—and neither do most of the dowsers it has to be said.

Of course, we all want to be miracle workers and many a dowser thinks their pendulum is bringing them higher knowledge when, in fact, it's just poor old JO pulling the string. It's best to be sure of your abilities if you're going to dowse whether the water is fit to drink or will give you dysentery! Personally, I wouldn't put great faith in my pendulum if I had to make such a judgement. If the circumstances were desperate, however, and I had to choose the only path out of the wilderness I might use the pendulum and just pray my Aumakua took pity on me!

In the hands of the expert, however, information from dowsing can be of real practical importance; apart from dowsing for water, oil or minerals, some of the energies given off from the earth which can be dowsed are good or bad for your health. In Germany—where dowsing is given some of the respect and attention it deserves—areas where earth energies cause outbreaks of cancer, cancer streets and cancer districts, have been discovered by dowsing. Incidentally, once the expert dowser gets to work, energy lines and energy risers are revealed as a hugely complicated subject involving good energies from ley lines, bad energies from ley lines polluted by a cell phone mast or a cemetery, good energy from spring water rising, bad energy from exhausted water sinking, not to mention risers and downers of an obscure origin.

A riser is fountain of energy rising up from the earth and can be bad for you although the Low Self of some people might be attracted to the riser to such an extent they place their beds or chairs over the hot spot. A local vicar died of cancer and one alternative therapist thought that this happened because he was attracted to such risers and would sleep on them.

Some risers curve back into the ground as a downer. Standing on a downer you can feel your energy being sucked out of you if you're sensitive like me. You can dowse your house and find what energies are rising in it and whether they're good or bad for you. You might find dowsing rods which cross over at a riser makes locating it easier. If you find a riser and don't trust your pendulum to tell you whether it's good or bad then do as I do; stand on the riser and get a friend to press your outstretched palm as in Exercise 1. If your arm goes all floppy then it's bad for you.

Join a dowsing group. They're full of psychically aware people and psychically aware people are smart people.

Whether your pendulum has access to special knowledge through the High Self or not, your JO is certainly swinging it. Hence at the very least we have an extremely useful tool for talking directly to JO even if he or she can only answer 'Yes', 'No' or 'Don't know'.

You might use the pendulum to find the special name your Low Self really likes.

It was once thought dangerous for others to know your name as this would enable them to put spells on you or hypnotize you. Suppose you want to find a new, special name for your Low Self that he or she down there really likes.

Swing the pendulum to and fro and slowly ask, "Do you want to be called Barbara . . . Margaret . . . Bridget . . . Bonny . . . Kylie . . . Boudicca?" And when you come to a name the pendulum approves of it will swing clockwise. If the Low Self wants to be called Boudicca then Boudicca it is.

It's also nice for the Clever One to have a shared secret with JO. It's a good start for developing that crucial relationship into one of trust. There's no end to the questions you can ask JO. Are you happy? Are you unhappy because of X? Do you really like Y? If not, is it because of A, B or C? Would you like to bring me a memory from March 1980 and I'll give you a chocolate? Do I need to take more vitamin C? Yes? Do I need to take 1 gram daily? . . . 2 grams? . . . 3 grams, OK.

Modern life with its distracting noise, its flashing, attention-grabbing media can obliterate our subtle, inner voice. If you've got a mobile phone then the world has its hypnotic hook into your mind at all times. It's most important to listen to the Low Self, however, as JO can have vital information for you, information no cell phone is going to provide and dowsing is the most scientific method of accessing this information.

All psychic tasks are best carried out in a laid-back, relaxed frame of mind. Just chill out and do it. You want to read someone's mind. Relax, think of them and doodle a few ideas and see what you come up with.

If your dowsing skills can access the High Self then dowsing becomes a fascinating ability with many medical and practical uses. It can also become a mystic practice. The dowser Lethbridge in his book, 'The Power of the Pendulum' describes how by shortening the length of his pendulum he could dowse *alternate universes* and derive information from archaeological finds!

Exercise 18
GETTING TO KNOW JO WITH THE PENDULUM

Here we have a very useful tool for both knowing JO and, if you have the gift, even accessing information from the High Self. Dowsers come to love their special pendulum almost as a fetish object when they develop a relationship with it but a button and thread can make a working pendulum to start off with. The following is not a comprehensive description of the complex subject of dowsing but a few hints to start the reader off.

(a)   Get some strong thread and tie a button or some little object on the end.
(b)   Suspend it on roughly six inches of thread and let it dangle.
(c)   Say (either mentally or out loud), "Give me 'yes' pendulum." With any luck the pendulum will start swinging clockwise.
(d)   Make it still and say, "Give me 'No', pendulum." With any luck the pendulum will start swinging anti-clockwise as if by magic.

(e) Say, "Give me 'Don't know', pendulum." It should just hang there. I think the 'don't know' option is important, otherwise we are forcing the pendulum to give a definitive answer which can produce misleading information. "Answer 'Yes' or 'No'," is an aggressive form of questioning after all and can force wrong answers out of anyone.

Dowsers say you must check before the start of every pendulum session to see that the pendulum hasn't reversed and 'No' become 'Yes'. How complicated life can be! Personally I haven't noticed this happening.

At this point it is worth noting that a minority of people find their pendulum doesn't move at all. It just hangs there devoid of life like a sock on the line on windless day. If your pendulum doesn't show any signs of life then your Low Self is very shy and doesn't want to come out into the world and play. If you can't find out why JO is so shy you're just going to have to give up on the pendulum for the time being.

If your pendulum swings then we have an extremely useful tool for talking to JO at least.

SEVEN
THE JOY OF HEALING

In that fascinating series of books about the Magus of Cyprus, 'Fire in the Heart' (Penguin) Kyriacos C Markides reported that Daskalos declared that healing is the ultimate proof of spirit overcoming the physical world as *no magician can heal*. David Copperfield, although he can fly around the stage like Peter Pan, cannot cure someone's big toe. Healing is the ultimate proof of spiritual power over the physical world and hence is given very little publicity these days. Healing is the ultimate challenge to mechanistic science which dictates the agenda of our society and hence is being driven underground. There are no famous healers reported in the popular press these days as the great Harry Edwards was in the 1950s onwards. The only publicity healing now enjoys is an expose.

What surprises life holds in store! If you'd told me as a university student of 20 that I had healing abilities I wouldn't have believed you or even known what you were talking about. I might even have brought some Bertrand Russell scientific 'logic' to bear on the subject.

My journey from the mundane to the miraculous was hardly a happy one, however. It involved the dragging weakness of a dreary, depressing ME-like condition. Several years from my healthy student days you find me gazing out of the dirty windowpane onto the main street of a Dorset town, gloomily watching an elderly woman hobble by and marvelling at the health and vigour which enabled her to get out and about and face the dank chill of an English winter. If I attempted to do the shopping on my heavy knees the dank air would send me coughing back to bed for weeks.

I am aware that there will two types of reader for the above paragraph—the healthy and the unhealthy ('Oh God! That's just the way I feel in winter!'). What a profound gulf lies between those who occupy healthy physical machines which work flat out in all weathers and those poor wretches who suffer from weakness or pain. If you are a healthy reader already yawning at the above paragraph do turn your attention to the High Self in the next chapter while if you belong to the unhealthy category read eagerly on.

I had an unhealthy childhood but became an active young adult until the mystery complaint struck me in full summer while I was living by the sea. I called it 'heavy knee' because there seemed to be nothing wrong with me apart from knees weary with carrying me around and a tendency to fall asleep. Initially there was a comic aspect to this but, over the years, the condition intensified . . . .

I could never depend upon my vitality. I might be doing something I enjoyed when all the noises around would become very loud as if the world outside had turned up its volume control vibrating the hollow exhaustion I suddenly experienced within. My kingdom for a bed! In summer I would be normal for a month or two and imagine my tedious health problem was all over. When we are healthy we can't imagine being ill and when we are ill we seem to have been ill forever. But every winter the condition worsened. Even my feet didn't seem to strike the ground properly as if my legs were mysteriously numbed. Only in spring—greenish, bloated and deeply depressed—depressed, would I emerge to rejoin the living.

What was the matter? Night sweats. Did that mean TB? Or just too much booze? I had chest X-rays, and, the help of an osteopath friend, explored every vitamin known to man. A multi-vitamin plus minerals course might fuel me for a week or two but no cure lasted. I searched greedily for the precious company of a fellow sufferer. "So you caught a cold in October and you still haven't thrown it off by March? Weakness in the knees and a dry throat? A weak feeling across the chest? Tell me more?" Alas, my companions of woe would eventually recover and leave me behind.

What was the matter with me? I learnt later that country friends were making their grim predictions about my future. "Ah, Joe can't face the cold, see. Don't think ee'll last many a winter more . . ."

I finally evolved a theory that I was a one-man germ-breeding culture. A mere cough from the other side of the supermarket and a germ would unerringly fly to my welcoming nostril . . . When I met those whom I suspected of harbouring a dangerous infection I fled.

During this deeply trying period, inspired by the sophisticated self-help philosophy of John Cowper Powys, I practised positive thought and tried to keep my sense of humour.

It was then my good fortune to find Max Freedom Long among the library of my girlfriend's father, and I was soon trying to increase my supplies of vital force. I was rather taken with the silly notion of accumulating knockout doses of vital force like a Yankee revivalist preacher. I failed. I read about healing as practised by the Kahunas but, despite my problems, had never thought that it might help me. So poorly is healing publicised that I associated it with an ineffectual holding of hands performed by old ladies in church halls.

Sometimes one's life seems to have been orchestrated from above.

My girl friend, Julie, had developed a Bible bump, that is a swollen tendon on the back of the wrist. It is named after the Bible because a traditional remedy for the condition was to place a Bible on the bump and whack the Bible. (A local doctor tried something of the sort on a patient of mine and it proved both painful and ineffective.) Ultrasound had been tried on Julie's wrist and a skilled osteopath with many years experience, after popping the bump back and it popping out again, said, "You'll just have to live with it, dear." This left the wrist painfully disabled, an unhappy condition for a highly active person trying to develop a crafts career.

And then, one day, Peggy, a local woman we knew, came into the antique shop where Julie worked as a manager and said, "I'm a healer."

"Go on then," said Julie. "Heal my wrist."

She laid her wrist on the counter. Peggy aimed the palm of her hand at the Bible bump and, as Julie expected, nothing happened at all.

A few days later the bump was flat and the wrist almost better!

Soon Peggy was at the house aiming her magic palm at my chest where it felt weak and the dreaded ME-like exhaustion lurked. I can still remember my first blast of vital force. There was warmth but more than warmth for the energy glows with love. And I took in a breath which seemed a different breath than that normally taken, a deep and profoundly relaxed breath, as if I were breathing for the first time. In fact, this is the relaxed, trance-like state which frequently accompanies healing. Afterwards I felt sleepy, but with a healthy, hopeful sort of sleepiness.

After a nap I discovered that in ten minutes Peggy had banished years of indifferent health. My temperature had gone for a start. I actually dug a pond that winter, a man who could scarcely go for a brisk walk in November without catching cold.

And then fate really took a hand in my affairs. Peggy came dashing round to see Julie in the antique shop, caught her feet in a one of those plastic belts used to tie breeze blocks together and keeled over, breaking her wrist. A few days later, while Peggy was still in hospital, Julie, who was a bit accident prone, obligingly fell on her healed wrist, raising the dreaded Bible bump again.

Until this point in time I had taken an open-minded though semi-humorous interest in psychic matters. My clairvoyant friend, Madame Bernadette, had demonstrated that clairvoyance worked and I became sensitive to unpleasant presences in certain houses, but this interesting phenomenon hadn't radically altered my worldview; I still believed with Bertrand Russell that ultimately science ruled, OK? I had tried my hand at Uri Geller spoon bending, thinking that I might be able to perform such wonders, but found I couldn't.

When Julie produced her Bible bump again, undaunted by past failures, I was interested to see if I could become a healer. After all, I had been reading Max Freedom Long on the subject of the secret science of the Kahunas. I started healing using the Kahuna method as described by Max Freedom Long.

"Let's see if I can heal you, Julie."

"Well of course you can't, Joe."

I raised my hand over the disabled wrist and could feel a faint sickly heat, the sort of heat that would make you shiver. In the morning, to everyone's astonishment, the Bible bump had subsided for the second, and final, time.

And I was reborn, intellectually as well as psychically. I was worried at first that I would have to stop drinking and think only pure thoughts in accordance with my new holy role as healer but fortunately this proved unnecessary. Some people, incidentally, discovering they have healing powers are completely freaked out by the phenomenon and what they imagine to be its religious implications that they never use their wonderful powers.

Thus began my healing activities with Julie as my healing test pilot, obligingly producing a number of complaints, including a verruca which dropped out leaving a conical hole.

My second patient was the healer who had changed my life. Setting a broken wrist properly isn't all that easy as a medical procedure and Peggy's wrist had set twisted and painful. I was able to help her.

Healing is compulsive and a healer develops tingling itchy palms whenever he catches sight of someone who needs help. I began to feel a throb of excitement if I saw someone limp into a party. Occasionally, after I had quietly suggested that I was a healer and might be able to help them, a person would fly away into the night, but I gradually managed to extend my range. At a party following a trade fair at Compton Marbling in Dorset I healed several ladies, all of whom were better in the morning. One, who had been about to buy a walking stick for a damaged ankle, went for a five-mile walk.

Once an acquaintance flung her lodger at me and bawled, "You're a healer, are you? Heal him then."

"I've had asthma since childhood," wheezed a boy with beautiful eyes.

In ten minutes or so his wheezing had stopped and after two more sessions he was skateboarding around town on a winter's night and reorganizing his life.

His landlady who had been trying to take the piss out of me failed to notice he had been healed as is the way of such people. The boy told me what a difference healing had made to his life (he had to adjust to a life without sickness benefit) although some people are so conditioned by the mechanistic fallacy of science that you can heal them and they still refuse to believe in healing.

After a deeply disappointing year with a national healing organization, I set up my own healing practice by advertising in a local paper. The healing I do might be described as the laying on of hands and I don't physically manipulate a patient in any way. However, a few years ago I noticed an astonishing phenomenon. When I was healing a patient's back the spine seemed to be moving under my hands! When this happens the patients sometimes report a fluttering sensation or even the pain of a bone being inserted in a socket. It seems that I have a psychic osteopath working through me.

The results of healing are permanent unless the body is subjected to more damage. Sometimes those with back problems need to check their lifestyle—many chairs and car seats seem to have been designed to make work for the osteopath.

Interestingly, the mysterious magic of healing doesn't involve hypnosis at all. I have healed patients who like Julie didn't believe I could heal them. Furthermore, I have healed patients when *I* didn't believe I could

The Kahuna Kit

heal them. In my early days as a healer a local woman I knew mentioned she had a bad knee. "I can heal knees," I said. 'I bet you can,' she thought sceptically. (The episode was reported in the local press.) "It comes from an operation on my back," said Wendy. 'I should have kept my mouth shut,' I thought. 'I won't be able to do anything if there's been an operation.' Thus neither healer nor patient believed that healing would work. "I'll give anything a try," she said.

Back at my house I put my hand over the spine where I could feel the cause of the problem existed (sometimes the source of the problem is different from where the pain, which is known as a referred pain, actually occurs) and Wendy felt energy tingling down to her knee. "Tell me when it stops," I said and after a few minutes Wendy remarked. "It's stopped, Joe. I'll try my knee. Good Lord, my knee's better!"

Despite having been on painkillers for months, Wendy's knee was instantly healed and has given her no more trouble.

Furthermore animals make excellent healing subjects and no one has told them that healing is going to cure their ills; this makes hypnosis an unlikely explanation.

I am eternally grateful to Max Freedom Long because it was by following his exercises on healing that I became a healer. One of Max's instructions was that the healer must have a clear image of the healed limb in his mind while healing. Of course, my mind like that of most people resembles a washing machine window and I used to worry about what would happen if a Dirty Harry type image invaded my mind while I was supposed to be serenely concentrating on the image of a healed limb.

I gradually discovered through some astonishing healing events that Max's Kahuna healing instructions were entirely unnecessary and I hadn't been using Kahuna methods at all. One day a girl hobbled in to see me with a condition that resembled rheumatoid arthritis. Her back had painfully seized up with no physical trauma having taken place. The doctor had put her on steroids, an energising drug that masks the pain for a few weeks, often leading to over-confidence on the part of the patient. As a temporary stimulant steroids are OK but they have side effects such as weigh gain and bone thinning during long-term usage.

I healed this girl and her back went hot and then cool. The healing energy is self-regulating and cools off when no longer needed.

"How's that then?" I asked confidently.

"It feels worse," she said, giving me an indescribable glance. "Like a knife being put in."

It's *very* rare that healing leads to the 'getting-worse-before-getting-better syndrome'. I had had one case before where this had happened; it had ultimately led to healing and I was confident that there would be a successful outcome now. In healing all change is change for the better.

"It'll be all right," I assured her. "Don't worry."

A few days later this girl was in her room when her spine started burning and she felt sick. She rushed over to the sink, threw up a pint of water and stood up completely healed of her back problem! At the time I wasn't even into absent healing and I was as amazed as my patient when I heard what had happened. I realised that I was a medium for healing, physical circuitry for some blessed spiritual agency which was doing the real work. Quite possibly I'd had the healing gift all my life and Max's exercises had simply triggered me into using it.

The writings of the great healer Harry Edwards were a constant source of information to me in the early days. All sorts of questions arise in the healer's mind when we become first aware of this wonderful gift. Can I heal myself? Will I live forever? Do I have to give up drinking? Can I heal relations? Can I heal people in a leather jacket? Do I have to wash my hands before healing? Harry answered most if not all of them. He had an amazing way with rheumatoid arthritis and could straighten out twisted limbs and used to hire the Albert Hall and film himself healing people. Arthritis sufferers would be carried on stage whereupon Harry Edwards would straighten them out and even have a little dance with healed ladies.

Once a doctor saw him straighten out a rheumatoid limb and commented, "I can see what you're doing but I don't know how you're doing it." "I'm not doing it," replied Harry.

I found this a highly illuminating remark. Although I haven't straightened out a twisted limb 'I' can heal back problems when all else has failed. I'm disappointed if there isn't an improvement or cure in one session and frequently patients walk away amazed to find themselves free from pain and surprised that they're not limping. I have realised, however, that 'I'm not doing it' but am a delighted participant in the transference of the healing power.

You would imagine, after successful filmed demonstrations by the likes of Harry Edwards in the Fifties, that healing would be part of NHS treatment by now. You would be wrong. The philosopher David Hume believed that if miracles did happen it was best to ignore them because they were too disruptive to a scientific view of the world. Once again philosophy was used to pervert rather than uncover the truth because, after all, if miracles occur in the physical world then they occur and have every right to be scientifically investigated. His hint has been avidly followed by both medical science and science generally. Just as valid psychic research proving the existence of the soul has been censored, so has the power of healing which rarely makes the news these days.

Though I have an inquiring mind, I'm so much in awe of the healing phenomenon and grateful for its blessed existence that I inquire no further into its cause, although the Aumakua obviously plays a part. That a limitless ocean of healing power for man or beast can be channelled into our difficult and sometimes terrible world I find profoundly reassuring.

Joe Potts

Exercise 19. THE KAHUNA SYSTEM OF HEALING

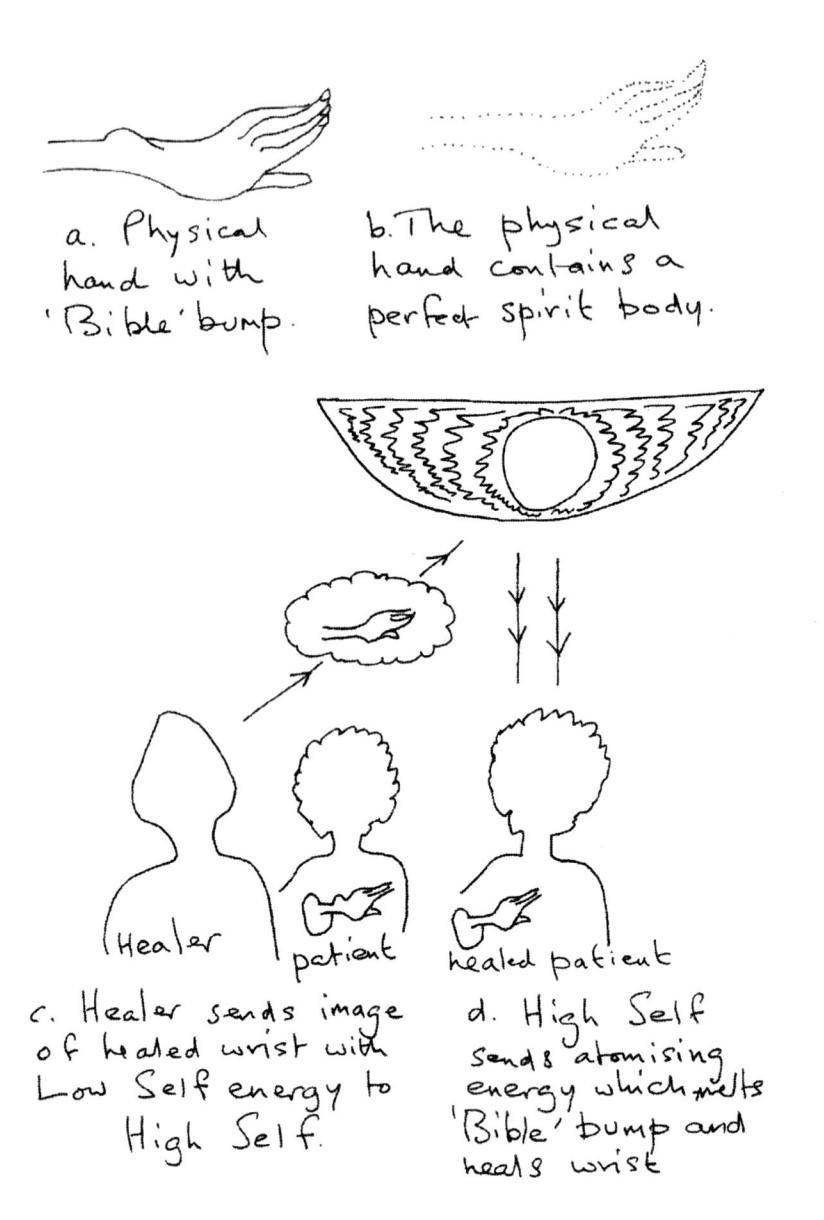

a. Physical hand with 'Bible' bump.

b. The physical hand contains a perfect spirit body.

Healer   patient   healed patient

c. Healer sends image of healed wrist with Low Self energy to High Self.

d. High Self sends atomising energy which melts 'Bible' bump and heals wrist

The Kahuna Kit

Everyone (apart from the odd misanthrope) wants to be a healer and Max Freedom Long confidently declared that everybody could be one—though I have since discovered that there was some controversy about this claim in Max's own Huna Research Association. Believing everything this remarkable researcher wrote was true I had a go and indeed became a healer.

The Kahuna theory of healing, Max discovered, was based on the idea of the spirit body. The aka spirit body is a complete mould, atom by atom, of the physical body. Just as an industrial process is able to project a hologram into a colloidal liquid containing the necessary metal and, through electrolysis, the image of the hologram will form into a delicate item of machinery, so the spirit body can mould the physical body back to health. Even though your physical body may have, say, a painful swelling, the spirit body will remain intact and perfect. Max claimed Kahuna healing was done as follows:

(a) He believed that yogic breathing methods just complicated matters. Boost your vital force by taking in three deep breaths to change your body sugars into energy.

(b) Lay hands on the patient where it hurts.

(c) Banish all thoughts of patient's pain, disease or anything merely getting better. Form a clear image only of the healed patient.

(d) While holding in your mind the image of the healed patient send vital force from the Low Self to your Aumakua.

(e) The Amakua will then boost your Low Self energy into mana-loa, the atomising vital force. This will dissolve the atoms of the health problem which will then fall back into the perfect mould of the spirit body.

(f) Hold onto the patient for a while, say quarter an hour, and see what happens. Patients vary remarkably in the length of time it takes to heal them—a small minority can be healed as soon as vital force is projected at them whereas with some a hands-on session of up to an hour is necessary.

Note: Certain healing books require the patient to do a veritable striptease wherein wool, jewellery, crystals and goodness knows what else have to be removed while the healer has to have scrupulously clean hands, wear clean white clothes and waft bad energies away into the corner of the room. Perhaps such precautions are necessary for some. Not, however, if you are a real healer. Harry Edwards, a keen gardener, sometimes used to rub a bit of soil on his hands as a joke before healing.

If you discover you are a real healer a mass of questions will arise and Harry Edward's writings are invaluable in providing the answers.

EIGHT
THE HIGH SELF
THE AUMAKUA Ow-ma ('a' as in map)-koo-a ('a' as in map)
THE GOD WITHIN

Fig 7. THE JUGGLER

In the first card of the Tarot the hat of the Juggler (like that of the lady in La Force) is twisted in the shape of the infinity sign ∞ representing the High Self, the sign of Universal Life. Note also the three-legged table.

'*O Man, Know thyself; In thee is hid THE TREASURE OF TREASURES.*'

Abipili, an Arabian alchemist.

Three souls—JO, the hysterical bio-computer of genius in the background, the Clever One that we read with . . . easy enough to take on board . . . but the Aumakua, the High Self, the God Within. A God within poor little us? Isn't God supposed to be the ultimate power and don't we feel increasingly marginalised in today's bizarre, atomised world? If we are God then why aren't we King or President or a rock star at least? Or why haven't we even won the lottery? It is an astonishing, improbable and bewildering concept to get your head round initially.

And yet, I suggest to you, spiritual reader, that you might already have had some experience of the High Self. Have you ever been overwhelmed by problems and walked away to some peaceful corner of the countryside and sat down alone and listened to the river? There, unexpectedly, a sense of calm overcomes you and your problems seem remote and not so bad after all.

Have you ever been blown away by a beautiful painting, perhaps a Turner sunset? Transported by an exquisite piece of music? The whole point of beauty is that it is en route to the High Self!

Have you ever been lost in the wilds? There are three paths of choice but only one leads safely back to camp. Although not a religious person you pray for guidance, chose the right path and find your way back to safety.

Have you ever had a difficult decision to make about your finances? You lie twisting at night, unable to sleep, worrying about this wretched problem which can make or break you. In the morning you decide to put the problem out of your mind for a week. Surprisingly, the answer to your horrible difficulty, an answer which seems obvious, soon comes to you from somewhere and it's the right answer. This is help not from poor JO but the High Self.

Have you ever tried a psychic exercise, perhaps trying to see into the future, and felt a strange sense of Love from Above?

If you have experienced any of these states of mind then you have glimpsed your High Self.

Aumakua translates as 'Older, parental, utterly trustworthy spirit.' It is neither male nor female but a parental God. Interestingly, alchemical illustrations often picture a hermaphroditic figure divided down the middle, half male, half female, referring to the concept of the androgynous God. Certain Hindu deities are pictured thus to this day.

This isn't a God who is going to tire of our perpetual complaints and blast us with a thunderbolt. This God isn't going to say, "Get lost, you whining, tiresome hypocrite, Joe." Just as our Low Self is *our* Low Self so the *Aumakua* is *our* High Self, *our* psychic future, *our* parental spirit. The God Within lives in a place of ineffable joy. It occupies a brighter and quite inexplicably blissful and totally illogical spiritual reality. Just as our JO looks up to the inconceivably clever Clever One, The Middle Self should look up to the inexplicable wisdom and splendour of the Treasure Within. The High Self is so beyond our comprehension, however, that a problem arises as to how to even describe or visualise it?

The *Aumakua* was sometimes symbolised as the sun or moon because both these bodies bring light and life (to the Egyptians, the moon was equal, if not superior to the sun as a fertility god) and hover above our heads; the sun shining down on us through a woodland canopy is as good a living image of the High Self as we are likely to experience.

Max examined the word *Aumakua* in its root meanings. '*Au*' meant 'self', 'meaning that it was *our* God and also 'A flow of water' referring to the High Self's use of vital force. The *au*, also translating as 'a fixed purpose', meant that the Aumakua was *unwavering in its higher resolve*. Whereas poor JO perpetually adapts to changing physical realities and the Middle Self is constantly rethinking its position in the face of new problems, the High Self is fixed and decided and monolithic in its purpose.

'*Ma*' is' to entwine as a vine' which refers to communication with the High Self by means of *vital force which can contain information*. '*Ma*' is 'the high point of a landmass', showing us the Aumakua is the highest of the three selves. Max discovered two other terms for the High Self, the '*akua-moho*' meaning 'the god who dwells with men' and '*akua-ulu*', the god who inspires men.'

One symbol of the High Self is the aura or halo which we find in both Buddhist and Christian art.

How to symbolize the ineffable, incomprehensible God Within? I suggest that the winged circle, containing the infinite, never-ending circle united with the heaven-searching wings, is a symbol of the Aumakua. According to James Churchward, Niven's Stone tablet 666 (Fig 10a) is the oldest winged circle in the world. (Niven was an archaeologist whose discoveries of buried cities in the region of Mexico City have been ignored by the establishment. As the site is 7,400 feet above sea level and the city was destroyed by a tsunami at ground level one can see why his findings, which require the rewriting of human history, have been shelved.)

The Naacal, Guatemalan, Assyrian, Persian, Egyptian and Greek cultures all have winged discs. Some of the circles have gods or men or serpents in them, indicating that these are the High Selves of Gods or men. As for the serpents—the winged serpent (Fig 10b) is a symbol of the energies of the earth linked with the energies of the heavens, of the energies of the *unihipili* united with those of the *Aumakua*. As above so below. It's quite simple.

Fig 8. WINGED DISCS AND WINGED SNAKES

a. The world's oldest winged disc

b. An Egyptian winged snake

c. A winged disc with snakes

Now for another extraordinary characteristic of the High Self. According to Kahuna lore the individual's *Aumakua* also belongs to a world congregation of *Aumakuas* known as the *Po'e Aumakua*. Is it possible for us poor battered humans, struggling to make sense of life, to contact the cosmic Aumakua, the World Mind, and the God Within and Without?

Strangely enough it is and this extraordinary experience can take us by complete, uplifting surprise.

In that classic work 'The Varieties of Religious Experience' William James (Brother of the novelist) quotes from the autobiography of a Mr. J. Trevor who, it seems, bunked church and found God. "One brilliant Sunday morning my wife and boys were to the Unitarian Church in Macclesfield. I felt it impossible to accompany them—as though to leave the sunshine on the hills, and go down there to the chapel, would be spiritual suicide. And I felt such need for inspiration and expansion in my life. So, very reluctantly and sadly, I left my wife and boys to go down into the town, while I went further up into the hills with my stick and dog. In the loveliness of the morning, and the beauty of the hills and valleys, I soon lost my sense of sadness and regret. For nearly an hour I walked along the road to 'The Cat and Fiddle', and then returned. On the way back, suddenly, and without warning, I felt I was in Heaven—an inward state of peace and joy and assurance indescribably intense, accompanied with a sense of being in a warm glow of light, as though the external condition had brought about the internal effect—a feeling of having passed beyond the body, though the scene around me stood out more clearly and as if nearer to me than before, by reason of the illumination in the midst of which I seemed to be placed. This deep emotion lasted, though with decreasing strength, until I reached home, and for some time after, only gradually passing away." Note that this contact with the High Self comes about literally out of the blue and much to the surprise and delight of the recipient.

In Exercise 21 I have a few suggestions to hopefully enable the reader to inch closer to your own High Self. Meeting with the World Mind is a joy so complete it seems impossible even as it lifts us totally beyond the lessons of day-to-day reality. I have had an awesome experience similar to Mr Trevor's.

I was leading a friend on a little pilgrimage which ended at St Aldhelms Chapel on the Dorset coast. I was familiar with the chapel—which resembles a stone tent near the lighthouse—and dowsed it. Most churches contain energy lines which cross inside them, frequently near the altar. Strangely enough this psychic energy cross also appears in stone-age barrows. There was nothing of the sort in St Aldhelms, however, which surprised me and lowered my expectations of a psychic event to zero. I could detect a riser near the altar but there was nothing unusual in that as risers appear all over the place. I sat down on a wooden settle to the right of the door in the aquarium light of the damp little chapel with its blackened pillars chewed with graffiti from eighteenth century vandals who, it must be said, scratched quite distinguished lettering into the stone.

It came upon me when I had no suspicion that such a state of mind even so much as existed. First of all I felt an energy which I took to be the familiar riser. But it was a *thinking energy* which suddenly and effortlessly carried me up and away to an altered ecstatic state, a state of raised spiritual consciousness of which I had no prior knowledge at all. I found myself bathed in what can only be described as a psychic sun, a sun so dazzlingly bright that my own frustrations in life, the stupidity and wickedness of human affairs in general, bewilderingly and quite unreasonably, *ceased to be even conceivable.* There were no shadows in the joyous sun which melted reason in its total empowerment. I sat there for several minutes and then, whistling Verdi, stepped out into the misty summer day.

The after effects of this penultimate spiritual experience wherein I shared the glory of the total, indivisible, inexplicable peace and unchallenged power of the World Mind lasted three days, during which time I felt both empowered and courageous, as if nothing, but nothing, could bring me down. The inhabitants of the town where I live had also changed. Whereas before the experience they seemed a boring lot now the phrase 'sainted beings' came to mind. I could almost see their auras and, providing they were just quietly going about their business, there seemed something strangely touching about them. They might have stepped out of a Stanley Spencer painting.

Then, in rather bizarre circumstances, everything changed back to normal. I just hope that I will experience this extraordinary state again some day.

This was quite the most powerful and uplifting psychic experience of my life but I have discovered that I am by no means unique. One of my patients experienced the Light while canoeing. He eagerly paddled back to the same spot next day and, of course, nothing happened. Naturally, I hurried back to the chapel but the settle is now just a seat as far as I am concerned. A dear friend of mine, an ex-GP who retrained as a chiropractor, has had the Light shine upon him three times. I'm a tad suspicious of those who claim to put themselves into such a state at will—although they undoubtedly reach a happy state of mind through meditation if they could switch on the Light at will they would remain permanently entranced.

The Indian spiritual tradition involves yogic techniques for accessing the World Mind or Po'e Aumakua. William James quotes Vihari Lala Vitra: 'That the mind itself has a higher state of existence beyond reason, a super conscious state, and that when the mind gets into that higher state, then this *knowledge beyond reasoning* comes . . . All the different steps in yoga are intended to bring us scientifically to the super conscious state or *Samadhi* . . . . Just as unconscious work is beneath consciousness, so there is another work which is above consciousness, and which, also, is not accompanied with the feeling of egotism . . . There is no feeling of I, and yet the mind works desireless, free from restlessness, objectless, bodiless. Then the truth shines in its full effulgence and we know ourselves—for Samadhi lies potential in us all—for what we truly are, free, immortal, omnipotent, loosed from the finite, and its contrasts of good and evil altogether, and identical with the Atman or Universal Soul.'

Note the yogi's trinity of mind: the unconscious (that misleading term), the reasoning soul and the super conscious. Just as there are those who claim that everyone is a healer the yogic teacher might well claim that heavenly state of Samadhi is available to all who practise the techniques. Until I meet a teacher who can enable me to do this I remain sceptical and I just have to hope that like Mr Trevor I will accidentally lapse into cosmic joy again, perhaps while taking the dog for a walk.

One element of yogic technique I have a problem with is the advice to "Stop your restless thoughts . . . make the mind a blank . . . loose all sense of self . . ."

The danger here is that if you succeed in making your mind a blank a passing entity looking for a physical home can move into the vacant space. I once healed a girl to whom this had actually happened.

"I feel very tired," she said. "And I feel—I know it sounds ridiculous—half pushed out of myself."

"When did this start?" I asked, suspecting a case of possession which can exhaust the victim's vital force.

"I was fine. I was enjoying my college course when I did these exercises for making my mind a blank. Then, after that, I felt tired all the time and half pushed out of myself."

"And do you hear voices in your head?"

"Yes, at times I do hear someone talking."

I healed her and she instantly felt better, no longer half-pushed out of her own body. Perhaps a powerful spiritual teacher of yoga would be able to guard against the possession of his pupils. It just goes to show, however, that we should be as careful with our spiritual exercises as with more lowly matters, such as drug taking.

Getting in touch with our High Self, however imperfectly, as opposed to making our mind a blank, is accessing *our* Aumakua, our personal Guardian Spirit, and awareness of this Higher Power can only raise our spiritual consciousness. Naturally, of course, just as we all want to be healers and access higher knowledge through the pendulum, we want to bask in the spiritual sun immediately. Unfortunately life isn't like that and we are likely to have sessions wondering whether we are actually meditating or just wasting time staring at the wall. We have to be humble and regard any small advance or insight as worthwhile.

Also remember that what goes up also comes down. Our spirituality cannot be raised permanently to new heights but must remain flexible with a constant dialogue between the Trinity of Mind. Just because we have been in touch with our High Self doesn't mean that the needs of the Low Self can vanish overnight. As the Low Self has to organise our health, sexuality, and food, if it took an interest exclusively in higher matters death would result. Indeed, some Indian yogis gave up life itself when they reached enlightenment. Others, on the other hand, use their spiritual status to sexually enjoy the young widow or anybody else handy.

Certain Christian advice seems premature, applying to the life beyond rather than the physical here and now. 'Love thy neighbour as thyself.' "All right, mate, here's the house deeds, hope you enjoy the place as much as I did." If we also 'turn the other cheek' to every bully and trickster in today's society we'd end up as homeless bag people unable to fight for even a discarded burger in the gutter. If a nation loved another nation as itself it would soon be annexed.

The physical world—which has a brutal reality of cause and effect often at odds with our spiritual aspirations—contains resources, such as water, oil, arable land, minerals or holy sites which are eagerly sought after and fought over by both religious and political organisations.

As most Christians have no intention of giving their property or wives and children to the nearest tramp in accord with absurd imperatives of their religion they can be left with a lingering sense of unworthiness and guilt—poison to spiritual development.

The Kahunas had something beautifully simple to say on the subject of God.

'The Grass doesn't understand the sheep.
'The sheep doesn't understand the shepherd.
'The shepherd doesn't understand God.'

Simple, clear and profound. In fact, when you investigate sacred knowledge such as that contained in the Qabalah (Jewish lore which reaches back into Ancient Egypt and beyond) one of the first things you discover is that God is unknowable even by mystics who spend 20 years starving in a cave. The Godhead is ineffable, inconceivable and incomprehensible. Our reasoning system founded in the physical world is based as it needs to be upon division and comparison and yet there is no division within the experience of the World Mind which defeats all reason and logic.

I find the idea of those who claim to be talking to God, the ultimate Creator God, very strange indeed, a form of cosmic megalomania. There is a God we *can* communicate with, however, and that is the God Within, the God the alchemist Abipili is referring to.

Hence our natural God-fearing instinct. Arrogant windbags like Christopher Hitchens may threaten to do to God what he did to Iraq but a normal person feels highly uncomfortable about insulting the Creator of All. The reason for our God-fearing tendency is poor JO, him or her below, *the Low Self who is likely to have had dealings with the High Self behind the back of the Clever One.* The Low Self, thought to be only interested in food, sex and violence, can receive important clairvoyant messages from the High Self or send vital force to the Aumakua. The Low Self, intimidated by even the reasoning ability of the Middle Self, is totally in awe of the High Self and understandably fearful of offending it. After all, the *Aumakua* with a whiff of *manaloa* could relieve the body, which the Low Self is tasked with maintaining and defending, of some terrible disease. Who would want to get on the wrong side of such a force?

And, of course, the educated Middle Self with its degree is blissfully ignorant of all this activity and sometimes ignores vital messages which are agitating JO. Our dogs, able to gauge the approach of their master as he leaves work to return home, are more psychically aware than many of us.

I have found my study of the Kahunas very fruitful indeed. Not only has it triggered me to become a powerful healer but has enabled me to rise above my troubles and glimpse, however dimly, the God Within. My few minutes of being surprised and dazzled by the glorious blaze of the World Mind have given me an inkling of a divine alternative universe infinitely superior to the physical dimension in which we labour. The Aumakua is unchanging whereas one problem with the physical world is that it is always changing and we are always faced with the prospect of health turning to sickness, sunshine to shadow or youth to age. In the physical world, no matter how young, healthy or successful we are we are always walking on ice.

In the *Upanishads* the concept of the God Within is a central belief underpinning the religion. 'Brahman is supreme; he is self-luminous, he is beyond all thought. Subtler than the subtle, farther than the farthest, nearer than the nearest. He resides in the heart of every being.' (Chandogya *Upanishads*) 'The Self of all creatures, the One Controller, who makes his one form into many objects, is seen by the wise to exist inside them. Such men and no others have bliss eternal.' (Katha *Upanishads*)

Just as a shattered fragment of a hologram contains the whole holographic image, it seems, according to this doctrine, that we are all fragments of Great Creative Force, sparks of the eternal fire of God.

The realisation of the Brahman Within is not a realisation of personal power and control as we westerners would eagerly imagine, however. The Brahman is within animals, plants—subtle, farther, nearer—and even objects—hence the mystic feeling of oneness with the universe—and is a realisation of humility as well as joy.

I had an interesting experience of practical help from my High Self last night (December 2006). I went off on an unnaturally warm but rainy night to deliver a lecture in the nearby town of Bournemouth. I had a map which indicated I should head for the town centre and branch off past the museum to my destination. When I reached the town centre I discovered that town planners and persecutors of the motorist had walled off the exit roads I needed. I parked outside the Town Hall and went back to ask help from two people I'd seen walking along in the dark. They had vanished.

I then saw that one of them was getting into a car. I asked the way and listened helplessly to the complicated directions which involved a huge detour back along the one-way system and the negotiation of countless roundabouts.

"But we're going there," said the lady. "You just have to follow us."

I followed them along a lengthy route. They eventually stopped at the side of the road and pointed out the hotel which was my destination. Its name in lights had been turned off so I would have driven past it anyway. I can't believe this help was entirely due to coincidence.

Such an event pales into insignificance compared with the experiences of a recent patient of mine. I suggested he writes his memoirs as his experiences as a psychic cop are so extraordinary. While a Metropolitan detective my patient would merely have to read about a particular wanted criminal and then, in an entirely relaxed manner, would go for a walk a day later and find himself bumping into and arresting the same man! At a murder scene in Soho he cast an eye over the witnesses and knew that a man holding a suitcase had done it and that his suitcase contained the evidence. Events proved him correct when the witness, now the suspect, was detained. Strangely enough my patient didn't regard his abilities as supernatural and had put it all down to instinct. He was fascinated to hear about the Kahuna system and the High Self having access to all knowledge.

When I'm healing I'm aware of a heightening of consciousness but I feel fairly normal. The High Self occasionally floods the healing experience with Love from Above, however, and sometimes phenomena occur which surprise me and confirm that I am a medium for a higher power. A woman reported that she'd seen me in a dream healing her and had felt better for some time after the dream. When she did come to see me in person I suggested she should have herself checked out by a doctor because she was an ominous grey colour and said she could hardly recognise herself in the mirror.

She came for healing three times and the last occasion was a powerful session. The vital force came through in such a quantity that she sweated while I myself was flooded with a feeling of Love from Above, a rare experience in my healing activity which would be emotionally exhausting if it happened regularly. At the end of the session she said she felt she had had enough healing for the time being and disappeared as healing patients do. What happened to the lady? Eventually I rang her up about a different matter and she told me an extraordinary tale.

She had been exhausted when she left me and in the morning had woken feeling dreadful. 'It hasn't worked,' she had thought. 'I'll have to go to hospital.' She had had then dozed and slept on and off for several days . . . and woken up completely cured!

Sometimes the Aumakua can intervene directly in human affairs as in the extraordinary events at the American Indian Pine Ridge Reservation in 1975. Why is it that 'Civilized Man' is so determined to eradicate 'Uncivilized Man'? It seems that we will not rest easily in our scientific beds until the last shaman has been either eliminated or made to see the virtues of a Western knowledge and education. At a place called Jumping Bull on the Pine Ridge Reservation 'civilized' half-breed Indians who had the backing of the government were waging covert war on purebred Indians who called in warriors to protect their endangered people.

These Indian warriors weren't muscle-bound Rambos but could do the washing up and change a nappy as well as performing their protective duties. The fatal events of that day are naturally disputed by the government but it seems that a car roared into Jumping Bull and armed men leapt out screaming. The warriors put down the babies, took off the rubber gloves, picked up something more lethal and, assuming their people were under attack, wasted the intruders.

It then emerged that the intruders—now dead intruders—were federal agents and the National Guard had also conveniently surrounded the reservation.

It was Massacre at Jumping Bull time. But the warriors did something most unusual. They prayed to their tribal god which was an eagle. Lo and behold! An eagle appeared over a piece of scrub! They crawled to where the eagle had led them, discovered the only path out of the trap and escaped.

A dramatic case, which the Kahunas would have found entirely natural, of contact with the tribal High Self and of prayers being answered at a fraught moment in time.

The existence of the High Self is not too good to be true. It is a reality which we can access at times.

We can all share our window of consciousness with our Aumakua to a greater or lesser degree. Sometimes a great artist can push us in such a direction. The sound of Louis Armstrong's trumpet, a strange bright, fat shout of joy which yet echoes with immemorial sorrows, can edge me towards a state of higher awareness. This is what art is for.

In a well-founded world in which the human race would maintain its place in the sun the High Self would be the ultimate source of inspiration for everyone and everything. Men of power, religious leaders, artists, scientists and the dreaded politicians would all draw ultimate inspiration and guidance from the higher wisdom of the Aumakua. In his book *The Way* Edward Goldsmith demonstrates conclusively that all great civilizations of the past had a sense of the proper conduct of their civilisation (Known as *Maat* by the Egyptians, for example) drawn from a higher source of wisdom. This morality would cover not only human affairs but our relationship with the environment. Goldsmith also convincingly demonstrates that our atomised culture contains no moral system whatever. The young have no respect for the old while the Church of England baulks at the thought of making ethical investments and the military play dice with the very existence of the planet.

Will the Aumakua once again make a significant contribution to human affairs? Certainly the concept can be profoundly important for us as individuals and if there's enough aware individuals we can make a difference. When I read 'The Secret Science Behind Miracles' I did so out of curiosity, not having experienced healing. Gradually, however, the Kahunas have taken on a universal significance for me. Healing really works and is a homely reliable frequently recurring miracle! Only the other day a patient rang me up to thank me for a single back treatment on worn discs which had greatly improved his condition.

Furthermore, I've deduced that the Kahuna system is not a magical code miraculously concocted by a few witch doctors in the middle of the Pacific but clearly relates to the Qabalah and sacred knowledge elsewhere. The Egyptians believed that we have several different souls, for example. The God Within chimes harmoniously with the Hindu belief of the Brahman dwelling in all things. I have been afforded a precious glimpse of the truth.

So best of luck, spiritual reader. Some of you may rise into the arms of the High Self with a few exercises whereas others may find it a leaden process where the concept almost seems a delusion. I don't find meditation all that easy myself. Spiritual development remains a paradoxical process wherein we need the help of the Low Self, replete with desires and fears, to contact the High Self, a psychic future beyond our comprehension.

Yet the opportunity for enlightenment is within us and we really do house the God Within. We can advance, however hesitantly, towards this wondrous gift and remember: the closer we are to the light the fewer shadows we can see.

Exercise 20
Controlling vital force

So far we have concentrated on becoming aware of vital force. Now we want to see if we can control it or send ideas by means of it.

- (a) Collect some vital force in your feet. Can you feel it tingling away there? Fill the body with vital force higher and higher, up, up, up, through the legs, the stomach the chest, the arms and finally to the head until you are full of vital force. Feel relaxed? It's a good way of getting to sleep, incidentally.
- (b) Got a pain anywhere? Direct vital force at the strained muscle or whatever is causing the trouble and put your healing hand on the problem area.
- (c) Aim the palm of your hand like the Egyptians at a sensitive friend and see if they can feel your vital force.
- (d) Think of a simple idea such as 'sun' and point the palm of your hand at a sensitive friend. Ask them to write down ideas that come into their mind. See if you can transfer ideas to them.
- (e) Reverse the process and see if they can transfer ideas to you.

NINE
GETTING IN TOUCH WITH YOUR HIGH SELF

Shine the light on me
Gospel song

Prayer, meditation and visionary experiences are all essentially a search for the High Self. As the High Self occupies a different order of psychic existence which defeats rational thought, contact is by no means easy for us ordinary mortals. I have found it possible to open myself up, however fleetingly, to a glimpse of my High Self, an experience which has been only a shadow of my St Adhelms Chapel spontaneous experience, and here are a few tips. Although, as a healer I am a channel for Higher Powers, this is a gifted process and contact with my Aumakua is something I have to work at.

If you a have a system, religious or otherwise, that you feel comfortable with, a system that means High Self to you—use that in making contact.

It's up to you and your inherent psychic talents and determination, visionary reader, whether *Aumakua* remains merely an empty word on a page or the seed of an idea that will grow and become the most noble and highest of trees on your psychic estate.

Remember: in contacting the High Self there is no angry, vengeful God waiting to hurl a thunderbolt in your direction, no dangerous astral spirit who will become incandescent with rage if you mispronounce his name. Your High Self, your Guardian Spirit, already exists as everybody has One. It is *your Aumakua*, and has probably already helped you out of some awful fix in the past. You're just going to become a little more familiar with this unimaginably beautiful presence.

In meditating on your *Aumakua* you are not trying to make your mind a blank which, as I have mentioned, can have unexpected consequences, but you are thinking of your own High Self.

Whereas the relationship between the Middle and Low Self is a relationship between reason and passion, complex but comprehensible, the relationship between the Middle Self and the High Self is altogether more paradoxical. The High Self is like a star gate into another dimension of higher consciousness. We can't comprehend it intellectually but we know that the powerful sense of love of this dimension can put our problems into perspective and surely leads the way to our psychic future.

How do you contact your Aumakua? The image of Buddha meditating with open palms on his knees offers a clue. He is sending vital force through his hands to the Aumakua at his head (See Fig 9a). Although you may not be able to tie yourself into a yogic knot you can still send energy through the palms of your hands while sitting comfortably. I am very impressed by those who *can* tie themselves into a knot and was astonished by the yogic flyers of the Natural Law Society. These guys—assuming that it wasn't trick photography—were able to hop like frogs while in a yogic squat. Some of us, however, could no more achieve such miracles than we could dance 'Swan Lake' on the ceiling. Incidentally, the Natural Law Society put up candidates for a UK election but the yogic flyers failed to make any impression on the electorate most of whom are schooled in ignoring psychic phenomena.

Fig 9. Contacting the Aumakua

a. A Buddhist posture

b. In the shower

It's thought that the flow of water makes contact easier and you could try an exercise in the shower.

A few words on spiritual development. Unlike many books on this subject, I make no claims that the reader will automatically be able to heal, see into the future or make successful prayers. Personally, I think such powers, if they are to happen on a regular basis, are gifted and need help from the spiritual world. However, some of you reading this may have a gift of this nature without realising it—just as I must have possessed healing powers without using them—and therefore it's well worthwhile seeing if you have been neglecting a wondrous psychic gift.

You will now realise that the word 'spiritual' includes all the violent and sexual urges of the Low Self as well as the rational abilities of the Middle Self. We can all forge a vital and happy relationship, so important for our mental and physical health, not to mention our social success, between the Middle Self and the Low Self. We can find out who we really are, what sort of animal we are. We can comfortably ride the Kahuna horse and we can be happy by simply telling him or her below how darned lucky we are—which we are, if only for having the strange gift of physical life! We can improve our Middle Self rational skills by working out what is truly in our own interest or, if we've got the stomach for it, reading the works of these strange subversive philosophers.

With positive thought and control of our Low Self we've got a foot on the bottom rung of the magical ladder. Most people's pendulum will swing and about 40% of people can sense vital force in my experience; in fact, most of the exercises in the book should work for more than half the readers.

It makes sense to assess your psychic gifts as you might assess singing: there's your tone-deaf person, there's the average person warbling in the bath, there's the pop singer, there's Tom Jones, there's Aretha Franklin, there's Domingo and there's Pavarotti. All these people are singing but some are more gifted than others. Voice training will get you only so far up the ladder. It's the same with psychic gifts. Take healing. Tell a sickly person that they're looking well, give them a pat on the shoulder and you've made a healing gesture and improved their day. Someone with the authority of a doctor could make a more lasting improvement with the same words causing a placebo effect. If you've taken a healing course you might be able to project your Low Self energy into a patient and change their mood for a day or two. It's still a long way from being a real healer, however.

I once met a sufferer from endometriosis (a painful woman's problem for which no conventional treatment exists) and briefly aimed energy at her. "That's just hitting the right spot," she said. I was surprised when she didn't contact me for a healing session. When she did ring me she said she'd been healed for three months! This is the healing power coming from some divine reservoir of love which surprises even those who channel it.

As for clairvoyance, we may well have an intuition about a friend that proves correct or be warned by our Aumakua not to travel on, say, 9/11 but that doesn't mean you can set up as a professional clairvoyant. It could be just a tip given to us by our High Self acting as a Guardian Angel. Possibly this ability can be developed with practice. Keep on trying hard enough and perhaps the gods will eventually take pity on you. Incidentally, if you consult a genuine clairvoyant it's worthwhile remembering that even they don't always get it right and you should examine that worrying problem logically as well as listening to their advice.

In the case of making a successful prayer, our prayer may be answered in a desperate emergency but that doesn't mean that our prayers will be automatically answered.

Personally I find meditation quite difficult. It's a paradoxical situation where we, our souls trapped in the physical world, can yet contact and be helped by the ineffable God Within belonging to a superior dimension. There's a tendency in all of us, especially when we start on the spiritual path—mea culpa—to think that if we understand a little about the High Self we can meditate and spring immediately into a state of nirvana where the psychic sun always shines. It hasn't been like that for me and I'm still trying to improve my meditative skills. But what we all have to remember is that a minutes' fleeting contact is better than nothing at all. My psychic development has taught me humility.

I don't intend for my remarks on contacting the High Self to be definitive. They are what I have found makes sense for me and undoubtedly some readers will have abilities which take them in different directions. It's an on-going subject which has been tackled by several writers. I highly recommend 'Urban Shaman' by Serge Kahili King. This book digs deeply into the shamanic world where the invisible world can overcome the physical—to the extent of even diverting a tsunami. He finds contact with the Aumakua easily achieved by thinking of something beautiful; I wish I could agree with him.

'Huna, A Beginner's Guide' by Enid Hoffman offers fresh experience, ideas and insights; one suggestion she makes is that the High Self can sometimes talk to you. The Aumakua is a vast and fascinating subject and further research is welcome.

Exercise 21
Contacting your Aumakua.

Various methods to try:

- (a) Buddha with the open palms of his hands resting on his knees is sending vital force to the God Within. If you're unable to tie yourself into a yogic knot try this method while sitting comfortably in a chair.
- (b) Note any movement of vital force.
- (c) Get some help from nature. Go to a wood and, with the sun symbolising the World Mind, pass vital force towards the crown of your head.
- (d) 'Aumakua, Aumakua, Aumakua' makes a very good mantra to keep the mental washing machine from starting up with thoughts like 'I hope I wasn't too eager with Mike . . . it puts some men off . . .' churning around in the mind.

(e) A sacred image to look at, such as a winged disc or a mandala, can stabilise the mind and check that washing machine.

(f) Getting help from suitable music. The climactic moments of opera, those moments when the singer reaches for the High C, mimic higher spiritual contact and you might try attending to these moments of musical ecstasy to put you in the mood. I once had a breakthrough moment while listening to Maria Callas.

(g) The shower. Strangely enough a shower is a good place to try these techniques—possibly because the water is washing away adverse psychic influences.

(h) To make a successful prayer remember Lady Tuth Shea.

(i) Make an offering such as a donation to charity as the Kahuna advised Max to do.

(j) Wrap a simple visual idea of what you want in vital force and send it towards your High Self.

FINALLY

How does our Western culture cater for the three souls of the Kahunas at this present time?

We have seen that spiritual matters are not simple, that spiritual development is not a case of climbing a spiritual Everest once and for all and becoming frozen there eternally. It's an ongoing dynamic of the three in one. There's the Great Organiser leading us to sex—not to mention sexcess—and power. Yet give way to JO and you can find yourself in a load of trouble. As Karl Jung liked to point out, "A man can fall in love and he is lost, he is gone, but he's fallen for the wrong woman."

A healthy urge to power, for we are all hard-wired to win, can turn a person into a monster who uses more and more underhand and violent methods to defeat opponents. A healthy urge to protect family and community can be so perverted by politicians that brave and noble young men can find themselves slaughtering innocents abroad.

At this moment in time the Low Self rules our culture. There is the remarkable omniscience of sport to which half of our news programmes are devoted. Ballism! It seems the entire world goes bumpity, bumpity, bump! If it's not 'the noble game' it's cricket and, if its not cricket, it's golf! If some evil demiurge turned all balls into cubes then surely half the world's population would commit suicide! There's nothing wrong with sport as a bit of personal exercise on Saturday morning, it's the sheer amount of pompous worship given to the 'the flannelled fool at the wicket, the muddied oaf at the goal,' to quote Kipling. If the world's population gave half the attention to the big ball they live on that they give to little balls everywhere then our global problems would surely be solved!

Entertainment caters almost entirely for the Low Self. Rarely does one see anything approaching the sly, cinematic intelligence of Hitchcock these days; it's all Big Bang with heroes improbably jumping through a hail of machine gun fire—whereas in real life a single round from an automatic is enough to send cops ducking for cover. The mentally-challenged male, seeing their hero cut down on movie A and being miraculously brought back to life in movie B, must form strange ideas about bullets and life and death. It probably seems quite a minor affair to shoot someone—as if the victim will reappear in a different movie.

The 20th Century was not a good time for the Middle Self for it was a time when people gradually ceased to think. In fiction, prior to the

20th Century, characters thought intelligently about their predicament and what to do about it. Dostoevsky's characters spend pages expounding their philosophy and fate. A major 20th Century turning point into non-thought and robotic behaviour is the work of Ernest Hemingway. Hem had a beautiful, rhythmic, strangely nostalgic prose style but never does a single Middle Self thought cross the mind of his characters whether they are about to get themselves shot fighting the Spanish Civil War or gun-running in the Caribbean—the guys just do what a guy's gotta do. They are robots, despite acute sensory awareness. Similarly, I don't recall any soap characters enjoying moments of reflection and wondering why they act as they do. It's more a case of JO on the loose. "Tracey, you bitch! If you try to get my John into your evil clutches, I swear I'll slit your bleeding froat!" Isn't our culture now a culture of sensation where both criminals and working folk just live their lives in a blur while enjoying the not inconsiderable pleasures of modernity. It takes the equivalent of a car crash to wake them up and make them think about the direction their lives are taking.

Bertrand Russell was a lecherous old man with a sparkling, wicked charisma about him. Unfortunately, as Wittgenstein complained, he was a spokesman for Mechanistic Scientism; but he was a philosopher at least and enjoyed huge authority so that he could even play a significant role in politics through CND. Russell was a national and international figure. The Middle Self Mind was fed with books such as '1984' and 'Brave New World' (which are even more relevant today than when they were written) and ideas still counted for something in the 20th Century, despite the Hemingway effect.

Is Dawkins, the present spokesman for Scientism, a fitting substitute for Russell? Dawkins simply endorses the spurious theories of his religion. Baboom! Baboom! Baboom! It's the Big Bang, folks, (Now being theoretically challenged, incidentally.) which somehow occurred despite the fact that, according to Scientism, energy can neither be created nor destroyed. Dust everywhere . . . a cosmos full of the stuff . . . which mysteriously formed itself into planets, folks, and, as soon as unique planet earth cooled down, with a little help from thunder and lightning, lo and behold, in the Book of Dawkins there mysteriously appeared on this planet what is recognised by scientists to be the most complicated thing in the universe . . . a cell . . . and this one cell became a load of cells

The Kahuna Kit

struggling among themselves to create the staggering phenomena of life as we know it.

The mechanism which created the wonders of nature is—wait for it–CHANCE mutation plus natural selection. A frog in a pond resembles a sunken leaf to fool the birds but what veritable sea of trillions of doomed frogs must have tried every disguise in the universe, everything from pretending they were wine gums to wearing mini World Cup T-shirts . . . all sadly gobbled up by predators before one lucky frog hit upon the leaf caper. And where is Mr Lucky Leaf Frog going to find Mrs Leaf Frog and breed froglets looking like leaves? The chances of her being in the same pond or down the road are non-existent! Presumably another trillion years of chance mutation would have to take place before the lucky couple were naturally selected in the same pond. Had Darwin had the faintest mathematical knowledge he would have made the earth a trillion-zillion years old instead of a paltry 4 billion which gives no time at all for even the Burgess Shale fossils to be formed.

No wonder Dawkins writes books about Darwinism called 'Climbing Mount Improbable' (You'd need a UFO to get up there, fella!) and waxes lyrical about the wonderful, breath-taking miracle of Natural Selection because it is indeed a miracle greater than a million Virgin Births that Darwin's daft, mathematically-impossible theory, can account for life as we know it. Darwinists are now breathing a huge sigh of relief and claiming the dotty theory to be completely validated by the genome project and even admitting how silly the theory of evolution was before the discovery of the double helix.

However, even if the scrapings from my big toe can produce the genetic history of the planet nothing is really explained. How did the miraculous one cell appear billions of years before it should have done? We have 98% identical genes to a fruit fly yet are supposed to derive from a common ancestor with monkeys. How did a monkey grandparent produce us—a unique creature capable of wrecking its own planet?

Dawkins is on safe enough grounds when describing the crimes of religions but strangely reticent about the manifold crimes of science. Deliberately exposing troops to nuclear blast, trying out radioactive iodine on pregnant mothers, boffins in the UK blowing noxious substances onto the coast, vivisection—our activities in the West are not that far removed from the terrifying activities of Nazi and Japanese scientists whose research we were keenly interested in, incidentally.

Dawkins, when not a credulous, peasant-minded believer in all things scientific, is the enemy of all psychic activity, including consciousness itself. One of his scientific heroes is the evil Skinner who tortured animals by keeping them in a Skinner Box, deprived of the 'irrelevant' sensory world. He even put his own daughter in one and drove her to suicide! This madman declared that all that exists is behaviour! (So where do the writings of Dickens, say, come from if only his behaviour existed?) It's a philosophy which should have had Skinner incarcerated in a madhouse but he is a hero in the Book of Dawkins. He's a scientist, you see, who believes that all that exists is that which can be measured and doesn't realise that measurement itself is an act of human consciousness!

Of course, we all want the lovely toys of applied science, just as we hope the deadly nerds won't release the technology from Hell in the form of, say, a nuclear war, but unfortunately Scientism is now the ruling philosophy of the human race. As for the scientists themselves... some of them, driven by intellectual conceit and a desire to find a lucrative place in scientific history, threaten the planet itself. Tesla himself, the electronic genius who had plans to bring free energy to the human race, cheerfully explained how you could put an end to the human experiment by using resonance to split the earth in half!

The Clever One has a bad time of it in today's world. We are told that to be clever we must believe in Scientism. While JO is constantly catered for by violent or sexual movies, sports, surreal advertisements and human-interest news stories, the Clever One is on a starvation diet. Most people will die rather than think and when they do think I sometimes wish they hadn't bothered. What more lethal thought-fashion was there than Communism? When Stalin was killing more of his own countrymen than Hitler killed in World War II and Mao had turned his entire country into a concentration camp where you could be shot for indulging in the bourgeois practice of friendship what on earth induced Picasso of all people to join the commies?

In Picasso's day, despite the inroads of what Wyndham Lewis called Hemingway's 'Dumb Ox', at least you were *supposed* to use your brains but thought has now become a mere fashion accessory. People adopt philosophies for no other reason than that they are trendy. How badly the Middle Self is served by the media! Take the recent financial crisis. Anyone who has invested in a property over the last 20 years knows that prices cannot rise forever. (There was a property crash in the 90's.) A financial system based upon property inflation is as secure as the South Sea Bubble. Yet the public were never informed of this patently obvious fact and Chancellor Gordon Brown was allowed to twiddle his thumbs and rattle on about 'sound financial probity' and declare that 'the days of boom and bust are now behind us'. If someone is planning World War III at the moment, despite acres of newsprint and cameras everywhere, the first we'll know about it is when the bombs start to fall.

And how is the High Self served culturally?

You can join a religion, of course, but, alas, as we have seen, religions become political organisations. Isn't it a strange idea that you can shed your crimes by confessing them to a priest—thus affording this character with employment and keeping at bay the terrible moment when the punters say, "Here, mate, isn't it time you worked for a living?" Too many religions create a sense of guilt, particularly sexual guilt, among the flock—thus blocking the path to psychic development. Sexual guilt is not a feature of the flock's cult leader, however, who frequently leads the life of a sultan amid the wives and children of the faithful.

Strangely enough, society throws up the unlikeliest figures to represent the High Self. Though only a boxer, Mahomet Ali became a High Self symbol who attracted the love of the world. This was due to his apparent ability to magically defeat brute force, in the shape of Sonny Liston, for example. One moment Liston was crushing his opponents as if driving a truck over them until he met Dancing Ali and was gently hammered to a standstill by the Louisville Lip. Ali's magic is partly an optical illusion as he has a large head which makes him look smaller on film than he actually is. Humour also helped him conquer the world. "Henry Cooper will thinks he's Gordon Cooper because I'm gonna put him into orbit."

Lady Diana, emerging from the British Establishment, became the 'Princess of Hearts', a Madonna figure, a symbol of High Self love and compassion. Humour was part of her character as well; she had a wonderfully defiant chuckle, enjoying life despite her many powerful enemies. Her mysterious death contained the elements of religious tragedy as many felt that the light had gone from the world stage when Lady Di was snuffed out. And, indeed, who is left these days to inspire us with their creativity or spiritual power?

Leaving world culture and returning to our own lives we find that we live in a world of paradox. Barely have got used to being a child than we find ourselves distracted by sex, barely have we got used to being young then we are reluctantly shuffled forward to middle age on the conveyer belt of time, barely have we got used to the shock of being parents than our children are carving out their own sexual domain. While such dangers of life as disease, poverty and betrayal have a horrible, intrusive certainty about them, life becomes more dreamlike the longer we live. Nor do riches free a person from all the shocks life brings to the suffering masses. In some ways it actually makes things worse—the rich have no excuses; if miserable then they can only blame their personal failure.

And yet, rich and poor alike, we contain in our High Self the golden seed of God, ultimate psychic wealth, the magical fragment of the cosmic hologram . . . if only we can access it . . .

How crucial it is that we bond with the Great Organiser and make sure this volcanic power has not been led astray by the siren calls of the media but is thinking what he or she should be thinking to achieve our greater good! Let us be as happy and joyous as we can be despite the shocks and surprises of life!

The highest Tarot card is the Aleph, the Juggler, and is he not a metaphor for us all as we juggle with our spirituality, creativity, relationships, health, money, sex, ego, society—not to mention the paradox of life itself?

So happy juggling, dear reader!

Aloha